A
Witch's Runes

A Witch's Runes

How to Make and Use Your Own Magick Stones

Susan Sheppard

A CITADEL PRESS BOOK
Published by Carol Publishing Group

A Citadel Press Book
Published by Carol Publishing Group
Citadel Press is a registered trademark of Carol Communications, Inc.

Editorial, sales and distribution, and rights and permissions inquiries should be
addressed to Carol Publishing Group, 120 Enterprise Avenue, Secaucus, N.J. 07094.

In Canada: Canadian Manda Group, One Atlantic Avenue, Suite 105, Toronto,
Ontario M6K 3E7

Carol Publishing Group books may be purchased in bulk at special discounts for
sales promotion, fund-raising, or educational purposes. Special editions can be
created to specifications. For details, contact Special Sales Department, Carol
Publishing Group, 120 Enterprise Avenue, Secaucus, N.J. 07094.

Manufactured in the United States of America
10 9 8 7 6 5 4 3 2 1

Library of Congress Cataloging-in-Publication Data

Sheppard, Susan.
    A witch's runes : how to make and use your own magick stones /
Susan Sheppard.
        p.   cm.
    "A Citadel Press book."
    Includes index.
    ISBN 0-8065-1996-7 (pbk.)
    1. Runes--Miscellanea.   2. Witchcraft.   I. Title.
BF1623.R89S54   1998
133.3'3--dc21   98-21911
                                                                 CIP

Druid's Crown

Druid, from the Sanskrit *daru-vid,* meaning
"clairvoyant of great skill."

Winter begins
when the bearded elementals
play their violins of sadness
in the trees. Some call this
wind which is only the virtuoso of bitterness
that turns in me always
where not one leaf is spared.

What I dream on in winter
is what I cannot have:
enamored by a bridal veil of green, faery light,
taken in by the gift of dark emeralds,
its mystery, the disorder and confusion,
grown to love the coarse, glittering hair
of the ascetic's groin. I close my eyes,
breathe *evergreen* . . .

Out of the forest,
I ride the white mare of midnight
with nightshade and hemlock at her temple.

I look up at the ashen clouds.
The sky above me changing.

The sky above me changing faces.
Women with horns. Men with paws.

I return to the forest and place the tree
of the everlasting tie upon my head.

It shall be green.

My wreath is the crown of lovers and sinners.
It is the crown of little gods and thieves.
It holds the starry blackness of a world
which falls away, and comes back.

It is fit for a queen.

Contents

Introduction

Witches have been associated with divination since recorded time. In fact, women, and men, who practice the art of divination were, and sometimes still are, believed to be witches. The very fact that one practices divination, or is a diviner or psychic, is to some synonymous with the word *witch*.

In fact, modern witches do not really have a divination system of their own—one that is based primarily on their history. (The exception is scrying, a common practice among witches that includes crystal ball–gazing or staring into mirrored surfaces to bring on clairvoyance.)

Modern witches generally read tarot cards (some decks are marketed specifically for witches), practice astrology, cast Scandinavian runes, or use the Kabbalah—a mystical Hebrew system of understanding that is also used for divination. Except for the runes, these methods of fortune-telling originated in the Middle East, brought to Europe by the Gypsies. The ever-popular Scandinavian runes may come the closest to the divinatory systems of the ancient British, but we will never know for sure because these magickal practices have been lost.

Although the symbols on the Witch's Runes you are about to create draw upon many sources, they were refined and gathered by one people—the ancient Picts. Using the Pictish symbols and alphabet is a natural evolution for witches who wish to draw upon their unique beginnings in the British Isles. I chose thirteen runes in the tradition of popular witchery that we see in movies and on television to create a coven of Pictish designs hand-painted on stones that contain thirteen unique energies. This appealed to me as an astrologer who understands the twelve signs and their twelve zodiac houses, plus a thirteenth "master" energy—one that remains mysterious and apart yet retains the energies of all the rest.

These Witch's Runes are unique because you can create them yourself. In the past, people who haven't been able to afford the off-the-rack runes have painted or carved their own. By doing this, the runes are charged or energized with the owner's own psychic powers. In doing psychic readings, you may come to realize that no divinatory tool is as accurate as the one you fashion specifically for yourself. By doing this, you can look forward to years of the pleasure of developing and understanding your own inborn witch abilities.

Now they are yours. Accept *the gift.*
Don't be afraid to call yourself *Witch.*

PART 1

The Witch

She walks in beauty, like the night
of cloudless climes and starry skies;
And all that's best of dark and light
Meet in her aspect and her eyes.

George Noel Gordon, Lord Byron

Witches are born witches. Individuals develop into witches because it is natural for them. The idea that women and men are converted into becoming witches by an ancient, earth-centered religion has no more credence than the notion of Christians being turned into saints because they go to church every Sunday.

True spiritual power is not a religion and never has been. Religion is merely a map, a reminder of some divine order that we are all a part of and take part in. Getting to the source, or the true nature of things seldom involves a structured group. The path of the mystic is the path of the individual. This is where witches come in.

It may be that true witches are simply a personality type with inherited powers and abilities, much like artists, other mystics, and healers. One might even say that witchcraft is as much of a talent as it is a religion, perhaps even more so.

Our need for witches as real or archetypes, is shown by the fact that when we do not have a witch in our community we usually create one. Perhaps the woman called "witch" is someone with mystical powers. Or perhaps she is, as in ages past, simply a scapegoat, an outcast.

We desire the witch and yet we reject her. We love her and yet we fear her.

But what does the witch really stand for?

Perhaps she is a reflection of our dark sides, our need to project our shadow self on others. Perhaps the witch represents a secret wish to use magick so we can attain power and mastery over our own fates. Perhaps witches simply represent a need to encounter the divine and sacred in our everyday lives.

Whatever your beliefs may be regarding the witch and her powers, you can be certain that her image reflects a need to understand the mystery and magick beyond ourselves.

You can also be certain that *she is real.*

Ὡιτϲηεѕ Τηεη, Ὡιτϲηεѕ Ποω

There is no one definition of a witch. Notions of witches have varied greatly throughout the mist and fog of centuries. Little agreement exists among those who have tried to explain the phenomenon of the witch and her followers, even among those who consider themselves witches. After all, the very nature of the witch defies convention.

British Witches

In the British Isles of ancient times, the image of the witch was quite different from what it was in other places in the world. People associated their witches primarily with faery lore, and the line drawn between faeries and witches was not clearly defined. Both kinds of creatures were considered supernatural beings. But unlike the fantasies of winged sprites and Halloween witches that we think of today, witches and faeries were considered to be very real flesh-and-blood creatures. In fact, the belief in faeries and witches was so strong in the British Isles before the Middle Ages (as well as long after) that some prominent families boasted they were descended from famous witch and faery clans. To be married to a woman who claimed to be descended from faeries was a position of high esteem for Scottish men.

Some women were believed to be faery changelings, a person who has been switched with a faery overnight. Only later did this turn into charges of "bewitchment"or of being "faery led," which sometimes ended in death for the woman, or supposed "faery-witch."

The concept of the faery as the benevolent, winged sprite that we have today is not the same as it was in the past. Faeries were considered to be capable of both good and evil. Among peasant folk, bowls of milk and honey cakes were often placed outside for the faeries to find at night, as an offering for them to not make their usual mischief in households—a tradition that still exists in the mountains of Appalachia today.

Like witches, faeries were associated with the hearth, the broom, and domesticity. Leaving a broom outside your kitchen door at night was thought to draw faeries to you. An unclean home also attracted faeries—the mischievous kind. They were often blamed for wrecking the house and making matters worse by hiding objects and playing practical jokes on the owners.

The Picts

Scotland was one place where belief in faeries and witches was especially strong, perhaps because Scotland was deeply entrenched in the traditions of the Picts, an ancient Scottish people. The Picts, a small-boned, dark people, were not like the other British tribes. They had many mysterious traditions and ways that were both exotic and suspect.

No one knows for sure where the Picts originally came from. Surrounding tribes believed they were a faery people with awesome, supernatural powers. After all, they were little and mysterious like the faeries. They spoke a language not related to others in the region. The Picts practiced fortune-telling, cast spells, used magick, and communicated with the dead.

It is thought the Pictish people were at first nomadic. Some have speculated they may have been Egyptians, Romans, or a tribe from Eastern Europe. However, the customs and the strange alphabet of the Picts were very similar to those of the Gypsies who came to Britain later. Many now believe the Picts and the Gypsies were one and the same.

Some letters in the Pict alphabet are recognizable as Rom symbols, that is belonging to the Gypsies, or Rom people, who originated in India and spread different eastern systems of divination throughout Europe after 1,000 A.D., when their appearance was first recorded. Both the Gypsies and the Picts were master diviners.

The Picts brought a unique brand of magickal arts to Scotland, including their own alphabet. But the Pictish alphabet was never meant to be a type of writing used to record history. Instead, it was intended to provide signals (sometimes carved in trees) for other Picts in their travels and also as a system for magick and divination. Part of this Pictish alphabet, or glyphs, are what comprise the Witch's Runes, which you are about to become acquainted with.

The Hammer of the Witches

Over the last five hundred years, rumors of witches as organized covens of Antichrists and underground satanists have been nothing more than lavish inventions. This all started with a religious treatise inspired by the Inquisition called *Malleus Maleficarum* or the *Hammer of the Witches*. Published in 1486, the *Malleus Maleficarum* was unique in that it accused witches of practicing a religion that was a rebellion against the Christian God that could have only have been inspired by Satan.

And yet most of the people who were thought to be witches were simply practicing a folk magick that had more to do with early European traditions than with any organized religion; what they were doing was more like passing down an old family recipe. It is true that these early people who practiced folk magic venerated the idea of a god (the Sun) and a goddess (the Moon), which they considered in harmony with earth changes. Many did practice sorcery. However, they had no concept of the Christian Devil up until that point.

In the *Hammer of the Witches*, all women were charged with being inherently evil, as daughters of Eve who had "gone out on a limb" and partaken of the fruit of the Tree of Knowledge. Women were also charged with having an almost diabolical "carnal lust," which made them easy targets for the Devil, whose main concern was to debase good Christian men by awakening their sexual cravings.

Questions posed in the *Hammer of the Witches* would seem like a Halloween spoof dreamed up by Orson Welles if we did not know of the hideous torture forced upon supposed witches as they were being interrogated about their dealings with the Devil. The real irony is this: Even in their wildest imaginings, few victims of the witch purge fancied themselves as witches. Many victims were simply the owners of land that the Church wanted. Others were isolated elderly women whose sins amounted to little more than holding conversations with their pets.

Some have estimated that more than three hundred thousand accused witches were hanged or burned at the stake with the explicit blessings of the Church during the witch purge. England and America murdered the fewest witches, while Scotland and Germany slaughtered tens of thousands of people alleged to be witches. In certain countries, such as Italy and Ireland, witchcraft was punishable only with a fine since it was considered to be of trivial concern and a small evil. But the Irish and Italian witches were not entirely protected and some were executed in both countries.

In many places, folk magick and other pagan beliefs quickly went underground. But the old traditions were still passed down in families who continued to honor and believe in witch and faery ancestry. Even today many English and Scottish people believe in hereditary witches.

Evolution of the Witch

As the early British tribes developed into nations, they began to form a clearer picture of the witch and her special powers. Most groups of the British Isles believed the witch to be something between a faery and a human. Like humans, the witch was mortal, but she was born with many of the same magickal powers that faeries were supposed to have. It was thought faeries were attracted to the witch for her special powers and would often do her bidding whether she was conscious of their presence or not.

Many people claimed to witness shimmering spheres of green faery light (as well as other colors) gathered around the witch's home, which left faery rings in the fields the next morning. Recent videotapes of English crop circles (mysterious patterns of intricate, circular forms which turned up in British fields in the 1980s) revealed glinting lights and mysterious orbs dancing and darting about overhead. Since the British Isles has the richest faery lore on the planet, one cannot help but see some connection between crop circles and reports of faeries and faery rings.

Witchcraft as a religion is pretty much a twentieth-century phe-nomenon that incorporates and borrows from shamanistic prac-tices, from not only Europe but all over the world. Gerald Gardner, a British civil servant, began to write about witchcraft in the late 1940s, making the subject of witches popular once again. By the 1950s, Gardner had formed a coven of hereditary witches. Later, with his assistant, Gardner penned a bible for modern witches called the *Book of Shadows*.

Around the same time, anthropologist Margaret Murray began to study the practice of witchcraft in various cultures. She believed that modern witchcraft was simply the remnant of a highly organized earth magick religion gone underground to escape the Inquisition. However, this may have been imposing twentieth-century views of religion on the witch. The concept of witches functioning as a group is antithetical to the private nature of the witch. The witch's solitary nature is part of the mystery that surrounds her.

Modern Witches

The witch has gone through many transformations and, until very recently, her image had been going mostly downhill. Witches have been portrayed in movies and literature as green-faced fiends, wart-nosed hags, evil enchantresses, the Devil's hand-maidens, those initiated into the sneaky, upstart world of the black arts and other kinds of negative projections that only served to uncover the shadowside of those pointing fingers at the so-called witch.

More recently, witches have been portrayed as humane followers of Wicca, astrologers, tarot readers, herbalists, peaceniks, ecologists, feminists who honor the ways and rituals of a female past, those who dabble in esoterica, and dark-robed eccentrics who aren't afraid to use their powers by casting spells. This is much closer to the truth, but not quite.

Witches and witchcraft, although related, are not the same thing. Since the idea of the witch is universal, it is inappropriate to say that witches are neopagans or Wiccans, as this represents only one aspect of the witch.

Go to any country in the world and bring up the topic of witches. While many people remain skeptical over the reality of witches, others are more curious and open—their eyebrows will suddenly rise and they will tell you stories of their witches. Usually, the story will center around an exceptional woman or man who shows remarkable spiritual powers or psychic skills. Sometimes this person is a healer or a visionary, able to part the curtains of the present that obscure our futures.

Of course, there will also be talk of magic and sorcery. Witches have been primarily associated with divination, which includes rune-casting. It seems that whenever individuals appear to have unusual powers and abilities, it is automatically assumed that they will invariably use it for their own ends.

Perhaps we can say that the witch is a gentle anarchist who isn't afraid to follow her own path. Finding connections between heaven and earth is her birthright. Divining the future with her Witch's Runes and charting the night sky is as natural to her as breathing. Drawing magic and mystery from the mundane routines of everyday life is her way.

The power of witches as mortals is that they live in a state of constant psychic awareness. Like shamans and priests, the witch has helped chart our course and hers from the very beginning. We can be assured that witches, as daughters of sun, moon, and stars, are with us now and forever.

Are You a Witch?

Definitions of what constitutes being a witch vary greatly from country to country and from past to present. Yet among those who believe in witches, there are similar witchlike traits that transcend culture and time. These traits often include being left-handed, possessing psychic powers, displaying a solitary nature, and having a close connection with nature and animals.

In the West, witches are portrayed primarily as women who cast spells or predict the future by using various forms of divination. In other places, such as West African countries, men are also thought to be witches.

The English believe the witch to be a psychic born into a family of psychics who, throughout the generations, have shown supernatural abilities. These are usually referred to as "hereditary witches," where the tools of the trade, such as reading signs and tokens as well as skills of divination and psychic interpretation, are passed down the family tree. Hereditary witches are not an organized group, such as a coven. They are simply following a craft or a way of life that is inborn and possibly genetic.

The idea of "witches born" goes back to a time when the seventh daughter born of a seventh daughter, or a seventh son born to a seventh son, was believed to have psychic powers or gifts. Since people rarely have that many children anymore, this folk belief has lost credence. After all, a seventh daughter of a seventh daughter would be very hard to find these days.

Those "born under a veil" were once thought to be witches. This "veil," or caul, is actually a membrane from the amniotic sac that covers the faces of some infants at birth.

According to the Romans, being born with a caul imparted psychic ability, blessings, and even protection from drowning. The Romans believed in the special properties of the caul to such an extent that many people took to wearing shriveled pieces of theirs as an amulet against evil. Conversely, the ancient Greeks believed anyone born under a veil would become a vampire, and thus, they were extremely concerned whenever a baby was born masked in the dreaded caul.

Yet the symbolism of the caul is important as it seems to suggest that the infant is veiled from the physical world and must first rely upon her psychic vision. Many clairvoyants say that when tapping into the psychic realms it's as if a veil is being lifted, where reaching the astral levels becomes a crossing over of the "veil between worlds."

Left-handedness has always been associated with witches and also with evil. Possibly this goes back to our basic human fear of difference. Of course, the Latin word for left is "sinister." In almost every culture, those with rare behaviors or abilities are singled out or held in suspicion. This includes left-handedness. How unfortunate, since the richness of our world depends upon diversity and the ability to view life in a unique way.

Most left-handed people would find it difficult to comply with convention even if they wanted to. Researchers believe that their perceptions are not quite the same as those of other people. Perhaps this is why so many psychics, geniuses, and professional ballplayers are left-handed. They seem to have the edge of viewing the world turned backward and upside down. Maybe it is because they can see the wholeness of life and embrace the richness of its contradictions, just like witches.

In the past, left-handed school children were forced to use their right hands instead of doing what came naturally for them. Perhaps this relates back to the superstition that surrounds left-handedness and witches. Many cultures believed that left-handedness was one of the physical traits of witches.

The majority of modern witches are right-handed as is the rest of the population. But left-handed people, dominated by the right brain or "dreaming mind," seem to move to a different wind than everyone else, existing in a field of flow and sensation. It's easy to see how this could lead to strong intuition and psychic ability. Perhaps this right-brained dominance gives the ability to enter altered states of consciousness, sort of an intuitive leaping of the mind, or a trance state, which is necessary to draw out works of art, poetry, music, and psychic visions.

Palmists know that unusual markings on the hands or palms, such as stars, triangles, and crosses, suggest an individual who is advanced when it comes to owning supernatural powers. Another feature in palmistry is the psychic M, where the main palm lines converge into an M in the center of the hand, or the inverted W, signifying a witch.

Like other visionaries, witches tend to have a solitary nature. There is a sense of mystery to the witch. In fact, time spent alone, often out in nature and among the elements, is an integral part of attaining spiritual strength and realizing your own powers as a witch. Thus, in nature the witch learns who she really is and finds her core of strength while not being distracted by the energies and intentions of others. After all, the witch is keenly sensitive. This is what makes her vulnerable, yet also strong.

As with other seers and mystics, witches have been said to experience significant or life-altering events around adolescence when there is a conversion to some form of spirituality. This conversion may be to some conventional religion, but most of the time it is not. After deciding on a path, the witch creates her own unique brand of spirituality that she works toward quietly or in a solitary way. This becomes the source of most of her strength.

Preferring moonlight to sunlight, the witch is typically a nocturnal creature. Perhaps this is what gives the witch her bad reputation, since we live in a world that associates darkness with evil rather than the richness of mystery. After all, darkness is when the unconscious mind comes alive and takes precedence over the less wise, conscious, waking self. No wonder mystic visions pour out of the midnight hour.

Midnight, or the "witching hour," is when the powers of the witch seem to culminate, for this is when she feels most strong. Why? Again, since most of the people around her are asleep, there are fewer distractions. In this way, the witch can be completely herself. Visions well up in darkness and the witch is able to draw them out and make them real. Plus, darkness is where dreams occur whenever she is asleep.

Psychic children who are especially loved by the faeries are often gifted with invisible playmates to help them cope with the loneliness or feelings of separation from those who are not *aware*. As the psychic child enters his or her teens, invisible playmates will be replaced by poltergeists or noisy ghosts in the home, making life for everyone else pretty interesting. Psychic activity will always follow these children, and yes, if made aware, these children can become witches.

Appearing wizened or unusually knowing as an infant could indicate a changeling, or faery child, put into the place of a human baby shortly after birth. The Picts and Celts believed witches to be faeries masquerading as humans. Witch children are said to show an impishness and a curious nature from the beginning. Their psychic abilities are usually quite apparent early on.

Such witch children and adults usually find solace in secret hiding places and sanctuaries in nature or other areas such as a loft or an attic room far away from the distractions of others. Many times the secret hiding places will be near a brook, a lush glen, a temple of rocks, an overgrown hillside or burrow, a river, or simply a quiet place where the subtle vibration of faery energies can be sensed or felt.

In the past, those with physical oddities or just an unusual appearance were said to be witches. People who were uncommonly beautiful or shockingly homely were also suspected of being witches as were those born with strange birthmarks. Even so, it was the eyes that gave the witch away.

Witches were thought to have an odd gaze or strange "cast" to their eyes, as if looking in two directions at the same time. Sometimes this meant that one eye was slightly out-of-alignment with the other, making the eyes appear crossed or giving a cockeyed appearance. Sometimes the eyes were different colors. A sharp or penetrating stare was also thought to denote a witch. This can be traced back to a belief in the Evil Eye—something many witches were said to possess.

In eastern Europe, those with eyebrows that touched or joined over the bridge of the nose were suspected of being witches. This probably goes back to the mistaken belief that werewolves were close companions to witches, since both were in league with the Devil. Hair on the links of the fingers or knuckles gave rise to rumours that certain people were witches or werewolves.

In keeping with this, anthropologists have noted that cultures where long hair is worn are often more idealistic and less apt to become involved in wars than those that emphasize short or shorn hair. Witches, too, are idealistic and thus, tend to be fond of longer hair. Some believe hair represents psychic energy, intuition, and original thinking, which radiates from the brain via the roots of the hair.

Long, flowing tresses symbolically keep the witch in tune with the abundant energies of the natural world. Likewise, witches feel especially close to trees and they draw great strength from them, as well as water, stars, clouds, creatures, and planets. At the matrix is the moon, which is at the source of much of the witch's power.

Of course, mysterious and paranormal occurrences surround the witch, since she is a channel or a vehicle for such activity whether or not she is aware of it. Many of these occurrences take the form of ghosts, spirits, and terrifying night visitors. In the past, communication with spirits alone was enough to brand a witch and send her to the stake. Even now, the appearance of uninvited spirits can announce the presence of a witch. Sometimes the witch (or psychic) is not aware of the fact that it is *her energy* that fuels the poltergeist and therefore, she is just as frightened over the sudden activity in her home as everyone else is. It's an eye-opening experience for all.

Some witches have telekinetic powers, or rather, they have the ability to move or affect objects from a distance without hands-on manipulation. Usually the objects will be electrical in nature, such as computers, watches, clocks, or machinery. Lights tend to flicker and become erratic around witches and psychics since their own energies can interfere with the electrical current or pulsations of the lights. Other electrical units, such as computers and television sets, tend to go haywire around witches since psychic energy is thought to be electrical.

All manner of creatures are attracted to witches, especially creatures of the wild. The continued reappearance of a certain animal, such as a hawk, crow, fox, or deer, means something significant as far as witches are concerned. Native Americans hold a parallel belief that if an animal appears in a dream, or is near when one has a vision or a life-altering experience, that animal becomes a spirit guide or helper. Such totem animals, or familiars, are said to aid the witch in her quest for spiritual harmony, for healing, and for developing psychic powers.

These animals can also act as affirmations or green lights, meaning they appear as signs to let the witch know she is on the right path, or in harmony and accord with the powers that be. The sudden appearance of an animal can also indicate a warning or a message of caution for the witch to beware. Rather than carrying out the wishes of the witch, animal familiars will act as guides and protectors from the natural world. Like faeries and ghosts, they become her companions.

Associated with the magick of both the natural and spiritual worlds, the witch is a romantic figure. In this way, she's similar to the artist—both wish to transcend the mundane and discover what is truly meaningful. In this way, they make their lives works of art, by choosing what relates to them and rejecting that which does not seem true, genuine, or affirming.

The witch remains a controversial figure since she chooses to embrace or integrate into her life the very things others run away from or fear, which include the mysteries of darkness, the magickal, and unseen worlds. In keeping with this, both artist and witch find inspiration and richness in mythic symbolism.

Even so, the witch is not especially impressed with authority or the status quo. Instead, she is able to pull spiritual meaning and psychic nuance from the routine of everyday life despite the usual restrictions or rules. Thus, the witch remains our mystical dissenter, our independent thinker. And this is precisely why the witch has remained in peril throughout history.

Nothing is ever abandoned by or lost on the witch. She takes what is there and makes it her own. She bends the forces of fate to shape, not only her destiny, but the fates of others. Through her skills of psychic intelligence and left-handed witchery, she gains mastery over her life, and also the future.

The secrets the witch holds can be deep, transforming, and fraught with danger. Such powers are meant for only a few.

Does any of this sound just a little too familiar?

Tell us, solitary seeker, are you a witch, too?

Origins of the
Witch's Runes

Like witches themselves, you will find the Witch's Runes eclectic. They belong to anyone who chooses to make use of their wisdom. There are thirteen Witch's Runes, as there were traditionally thought to be thirteen witches in a coven. Although there is often fear and superstition surrounding thirteen, witches use this number for its power and influence. The thirteen runes correspond with the twelve astrological signs and their houses, plus one—the Eye—which contains the energies of all of the previous ones.

The thirteen Witch's Runes suggest the twelve hours leading up to midnight, or the witching hour. The thirteenth rune, which is the most important, contains the collective energies of the previous runes. In this way the Eye Rune becomes "the watcher," a presence whose abode is the whispering woods outside the lunar light of faery rings. Perhaps this presence is ourselves. Perhaps this presence is beyond ourselves. Thus, we must cast the stones to know and understand.

Thirteen is a number of great influence. This is why much superstition surrounds it. There are thirteen moons in rare and magickal years. Jesus had twelve disciples whose personalities and fates corresponded to the zodiac signs, according to astrologer Alan Oken. At the head was the Christ (which made thirteen) as lookout, redeemer, and guide for the group. The Christ, as a master energy for good, became like a Druidic faery king who appeared suddenly to perform his magickal feats and wondrous miracles, then disappeared just as quickly, spirited away by the faeries and reclaimed by the Avalon lands of the sleeping dead.

The symbols on the Witch's Runes can be traced throughout the European continent, the Near East, the Far East, and Africa. Similar motifs have been found on petroglyphs (rock carvings) in the New World. Most of the symbols appear to have Indo-European roots, yet we aren't entirely sure where or when they originated. We do know that Gypsies used many of these symbols in their talismans and probably brought them into Europe during the Middle Ages after leaving their homeland of India.

It is quite possible that early Aryan invaders brought some of the symbols into India first and the Gypsies only reintroduced them to European culture at a later time. This would explain why a few of my designs are quite similar to the Germanic runes that were widespread in northern Europe by A.D. 100. But they can be traced back to a much earlier time.

We do know these Witch's Runes represent a divinatory language, a symbology if you will, of great antiquity. As sacred holders of arcane knowledge, Gypsies may have picked up the symbols for talismans that worked for them and discarded the ones that did not. Perhaps this is why many of the Gypsy symbols painted on amulets seem to represent a hodgepodge from various sources. Many of the designs were used in the writings of the Picts, whose name inspired the word *pixie*, meaning an elfin-like faery. This idea substantiates the old belief that human witches were natural allies of faeries and are possibly even related to them.

The word *rune* derives from the Northern Germanic word *ru*, meaning to remain hidden, to be held in mystery or kept secret. The Norse people claimed their runes came from Odin, God of war and wisdom, who screamed and fell down upon discovering these sacred Scandinavian symbols. Early runic symbols appeared on Nordic gravestones as a way of warding off evil spirits, and possibly of keeping the souls of the dead from wandering or becoming ghosts. Later, runic designs were carved into wood, bronze, and stone, then incorporated into swords, jewelry, ships, talismans, and other items.

The earliest runes, however, were not Germanic. They evolved from writings in the Middle East. Sacred amulets inscribed with hieroglyphics were called *wedjan* by Egyptian priests and were thought to be imbued with magickal and divine powers.

The Egyptians were very much involved with word magick, as were other cultures in the Near East. Ancient people believed that if you could name something for what it really was (sometimes by using its secret name), you could hold power over it. This included even their deities. The idea of words as magick developed into chanting, incantations, spells, and the use of talismans and amulets to ask for favor and protection. Thoth, god of writing and scribes, was held in high esteem and so were his hieroglyphics that inspire magick even to this day. It is possible that the Gypsies, who touted themselves as "Egyptians," helped pave the way for magickal runes to be used much later in Europe.

The three celestial runes—sun, moon, and star—are without a doubt the most recognizable as modern witch symbols. Magick has always been linked to the sky, and witches with flight. The Goddess Ishtar of Babylonia may have inspired the Star Rune. She was called not only the Queen of Heaven, and Queen of Oracles, but also the "Star adored by her lovers."

But Ishtar isn't the only religious figure adored in the image of a star. Around 2 B.C., a conjunction of the planets Jupiter and Mars formed what appeared to be a very bright star in the eastern skies. Babylonian astrologers recognized the lights as Jupiter, the star of kings; and Mars, as the star of Palestine. It was then that the Magi astrologers went in search of an infant King, later known as the Christ child. Had the Magi not been astrologers, or Babylonian, they would not have considered this lineup of stars particularly significant. But these ancients knew that stars were magickal.

While the Egyptians favored the six-pointed star by painting it on the ceilings of their temples, the Babylonians used the eight-pointed variety.

In many cultures, the Star Rune has been associated with speculation and even adoration. It's as if the distant star holds within its points our wishes and dreams, representing what we long for.

The Gypsies seemed to be most fond of the Sun, Star, and Moon Runes, which is probably why we associate these primary symbols with divination, but it goes even deeper than that. American Gypsies divide themselves into four different nations or tribes. The Machwaya Gypsies are associated with the Sun and are aristrocrats among the Rom. The Lowara Gypsies consider themselves ruled by the Moon and have special occult powers. The Kalderdasha are associated with stars and make the finest fortune-tellers. Churara Gypsies are ruled by the dagger.

There is little doubt that the Gypsies are the keepers of the flame as far as modern divination is concerned, and their symbols are important. Perhaps this is the reason Sun, Moon, and Star designs are so often read as signs for fortune-telling.

How do witches figure in? Because witches are primarily domestic and solitary, they are resourceful. They make use of whatever is available. Perhaps this is why the witch is adept at so many forms of divination. After all, traditional European witch-craft's tie to the Gypsies has always been a strong one. This also holds true for witchcraft and divination in Russia and the Middle East.

Yet the witch works from the perspective of the individual. No one owns her special brand of magick and spirituality. The Witch's Runes are hers but others can use them. The witch remains fluid in her beliefs. Perhaps this has something to do with her reputation as astral traveler and shape-shifter.

While Wicca and ritual witchcraft have the elements of a religion, being a witch does not. But the witch honors all of the spiritual traditions that have preceded her. She takes what works for her and makes use of its meanings. Most important, the witch always gives back.

PART 2

how to Choose
and Make your
Own Runes

From Magick Stones to Runes

The most powerful divinatory tools are the ones you make yourself. Whenever you put your own power and focus into anything, it retains much of your energy. Rocks from the natural world around you make good Witch's Runes since you are already in harmony with these elements.

It takes no special artistry to create your own set of runes. You can begin by going outside to find some suitable stones. You will need thirteen rocks of a similar size with a surface flat enough to paint on. Perhaps you will find your magick stones in your driveway or along a path—perhaps in a secret place of yours in the woods. Stones that have been smoothed by water are especially flawless and beautiful. You can find these near rivers, lakes, or creek beds, even in cemeteries and mall parking lots!

You will want to search out rocks that are approximately the size of a half-dollar. Smaller rocks are difficult to hold on to while painting. Search for flat surfaces rather than rounded ones as these are easier to paint on. Avoid big rocks with rough, grainy surfaces. The basic shape of the stones will vary but try to choose ones of the same general size and weight. This will take a little while, as you'll be amazed at how different and varied plain old rocks can be.

Hold each rock between your thumb and index finger for a few moments. See if the stone agrees with you and if you like its energy. If the rock starts to feel satiny or almost slippery between your fingers, it is a good rock to use. If you feel a buzz of energy, sort of like an electrical shock, this also indicates a perfect stone.

As you select your stones, you will want to pick out some extra rocks to test your abilities on. Put your rocks in a cloth sack or a basket and take them home. Immediately place the rocks in a bucket and fill it with cold water. Rinse them very slowly and gently. To purify the rocks further, add a dash of salt. If you like, you can steep them in your favorite herb, perhaps lavender or chamomile.

After your stones have been cleansed, you may want to place them under moonlight for a night or two. Since moons are for mystics, any moon will do! A full moon is ideal. A new moon is great, too. But if you're a creature of the moment, you'll probably want to get to work on your runes right away.

Make certain there is no excess mud or gravel on the rocks, but don't bother trying to get them 100 percent clean. Dry your stones with a paper towel or put them up high so they'll dry faster. As soon as their surfaces feel smooth and they are completely dry, it is time to begin painting your runes.

Getting Ready to Paint

Look for acrylic or fabric paints at a store which sells art supplies. For now, choose flat colors and not glossy paints. The colors you will need are:

Lamp Black
Basic White
Any color of your choice
Antique gold or silver

Pick up some good brushes while you are there. By this I mean the kind professional artists use and not the cheap ones children paint model cars with. You will need three brushes.

Number 0 brush
Number 1 brush
Number 10 flat brush

Your number 0 brush is for painting details and should be almost as fine as a human eyelash. Your number 1 brush is used to fill in and correct your mistakes. Your number 10 flat brush is used for painting the surfaces.

You will also need to buy some *round* multipurpose tabs usually sold in the office supply section of your store. These tabs will help you create a perfect circle on your runes and can save you a lot of frustration and work.

When painting the runes, three colors are used. Black makes up the background. The symbols on the stones are painted with white and another color that you choose for the rest of the stone. The color you decide to paint your runes is ultimately up to you and will reflect your unique sense of magic and enchantment. But certain colors work better than others because they have more to do with a sense of mystery and drama.

Atmospheric tones always evoke a sense of the mystical. These include all shades of blue ranging from turquoise to indigo. Navy, royal, cobalt, and sky blue reflect the many phases and changes in the sky. Woodsy greens and burgundy shades also work well. Leaving the runes black while highlighting certain designs in metallic tones can create dramatic effects.

Purple is a wonderful choice for the Witch's Runes. One word of advice though. You would do best to select your favorite color of purple at the paint counter. If you're into mixing colors, you probably already know that red mixed with blue makes purple. Well, at least they're supposed to. A pure, vibrant shade of purple is quite difficult to achieve. Generally, if you mix blue with red, you end up with a yucky shade of brownish purple. If you mix white with it, you get a dirty mauve. Not a pretty picture. So pick up your favorite shade of purple at the art store. When painting your runes, mix a smidgen of white with purple or else it will be too dark.

Painting Your Stones

Find a painting space and spread out some sheets of white paper. If you can find paper with a waxy surface, that will be ideal. If you must use newsprint paper, keep turning your runes as they dry or else they will pick up some of the fiber and will stick to the paper.

Take a flat brush and paint all of your runes a solid black. Allow the rocks to dry for thirty minutes.

After the black paint has dried, take your smallest paintbrush and draw a circle on the flattest parts of your rocks. You can draw this circle freely, or you can trace a quarter on a piece of paper, then cut out this circle and use it as a pattern.

Allow this coat of paint to dry thoroughly, for about thirty to forty minutes. As soon as the paint is dry, you can begin painting your runic symbols. If you have used paper cutouts to make your circle, remove them carefully. If the outside paint flakes away or rips as you pull away the paper, smooth the paint down with your fingertip. The paint normally adheres easily to the rock.

Painting the Runic Symbols

All drawing consists of straight and curving lines. True in all art, this is especially true when it comes to runes and hieroglyphics.

Before starting, put a dab of white paint on your palette. Roll the tip of your tiniest brush in the paint. Do not glob the paint on your brush. Remember—the tip of your brush should be almost as fine as an eyelash!

Ready to start? We shall begin with the Sun Rune.

SUN RUNE

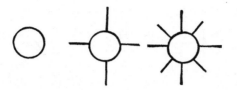

Draw a circle. Add these four lines. Now paint shorter lines. And there you have it. The Sun Rune.

MOON RUNE

Draw this curve. Curve your line upward. Bring line to a point. No mystery now. You have the Moon Rune.

FLIGHT RUNE

Paint a bird with wavy lines. Make another. Then a smaller one. You end up with three birds. You have your Flight Rune.

RINGS RUNE

Draw a circle. And another circle. Then another circle. You have made your connection. You have the Rings Rune.

ROMANCE RUNE

Paint this curve. And another curve until it looks like a fish standing on its tail. Complete a half circle joining them all. This rune is essential. It is the Romance Rune.

WOMAN RUNE

Draw this line. Another one to form the female V. Add a line. This familiar shape becomes the Woman Rune.

MAN RUNE

Paint this line. Another line forms an arrow. Add a thrust. This symbol relates energy and is called the Man Rune.

HARVEST RUNE

Paint this design. Add lines and details. Make several dots. Watch this rune flower. It is called the Harvest Rune.

CROSSROADS RUNE

Draw a simple cross. Add arrows. Add two more arrows. You have made your direction. Call this the Crossroads Rune.

STAR RUNE

Draw a simple cross. Add a diagonal line. Paint another diagonal. Now you can shed light on your reading. You have the Star Rune.

WAVES RUNE

Follow the spiral. Curve until your rune looks like this. Expect to plumb the depths. You have painted the Waves Rune.

SCYTHE RUNE

Recreate this curve. Draw a tail. Add this bar. Now you're hooked. You've made yourself a Scythe Rune.

EYE RUNE

Paint a white fish. Add a black circle to make an eye. Paint in the color of the iris. Leave the pupil. Add two dots of light.

Your second sight is real. The last one is the Eye Rune.

Not getting your details to your liking? Don't worry. All you have to do is paint over your messed-up rune with black paint and start all over again. Or you can take a pen and practice on a sheet of paper until you get the hang of rune painting.

Oftentimes when the rune seems difficult to paint, it may mean the surface of your stone is too rough or uneven. When in doubt, go out and find a smoother stone.

As soon as you are satisfied with your painting of the runes, it is time to decorate your rocks and make them yours. Metallic paints can really add sparkle to your stones. You can start out by reiterating the circle around your runic symbol to draw it out even more. Use a careful hand to make your line even. After you have surrounded your circle with gold, copper, or silver, you can paint sunbursts, zigzags, stripes or the entire rune in metallic paints.

You can't go wrong when painting your rocks in metallic tones. It's easier and the runes look dramatic and grab attention no matter what you do. You can varnish your rocks if you like, but this is not necessary. In fact, flat, unvarnished surfaces make a more dramatic statement in contrast to gold or silver.

Now that you are happy with your results, it is time to set the runes aside and go to work on the cloth bag to hold your stones.

how to Make your Own Rune Bag

Find pieces of material that are complimentary to your painted runes. You will want to pick out a sturdy cotton-based fabric rather than silky materials or velvets, which are difficult for novices to handle.

If you want to put a lining in your bag, pick out a design or a solid piece of material that matches the fabric for the bag. Cotton is a good choice here as well.

Cut your fabric into a rectangular shape approximately 9 × 12 inches. (This is slightly larger than a typical piece of typing paper.) Place your two fabrics together with the designs facing *into* each other. Pin the pieces together.

Stitch your fabric pieces together with small strokes, leaving one side of your rectangle open. Leave an open space slightly over one inch long on one side as well. You will need to work your draw-string through this later or you won't be able to open and close your bag.

Turn your bag inside out, bringing the designs or print that you wish to show to the outside. In order to keep the edges of your bag straight, it's a good idea to press the wrinkles out either by using an iron or even your hand. Some like to use straight pins to hold the pieces of fabric together.

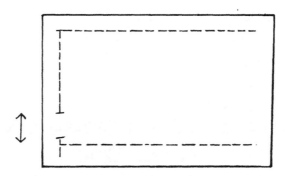

As soon as you have your pieces of material the way you want them to be, you can stitch the edges of your bag together either by hand or by sewing machine. You will want to make a channel by making two separate rows of stitching across the top of your bag. This channel should be large enough to pull your drawstring through later.

When sewing is completed, your fabric pieces should look like this:

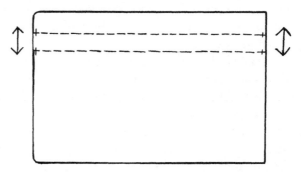

Fold your bag over. Turn the pouch to the side that you want to show and then smooth down the fabric with your hand.

Next find a safety pin. Attach the safety pen to the end of what will be your string. (A thin velvet ribbon or suede cord creates a good, durable drawstring.) You will need about a half-yard of string or cord.

Using your pin as a guide, work the string through the channel you created for your bag. As soon as you come to the opening in the side of your bag, pull gently and tie the end of your drawstring in a knot. The pouch in which you keep your Witch's Runes should look something like this:

If you aren't certain about your sewing skills, many specialty shops and craft stores sell drawstring pouches in various sizes and styles. But in a pinch, you can use a bag of any kind. Even plastic or paper bags can work out just fine.

PART 3

Interpreting
Your Runes

Reading the Witch's Runes is easy once you begin to understand their meanings. There are thirteen runes in all, and each one has its own interpretation based upon various sources. These include Rom and Pictish symbols, old faery lore, astrological signs and their guiding planets, gods and goddesses, and elemental forces.

A basic understanding of the astrological signs could potentially enrich your psychic rune reading. (Included is a chart of the runes and their planetary and sign correspondences. See page 92.) However, a knowledge of astrology isn't necessary in reading the Witch's Runes.

If this sounds complicated, it isn't. Doing a reading with the Witch's Runes is as simple as pulling a rock out of a bag and looking up its meaning in the text. Once you become familiar with the runes you can try more complicated and involved readings for yourself and your friends.

There are several reading methods given in this book but they are only suggestions. It's just as valid if you make up methods of your own. This allows you to be creative and spontaneous, and therefore, more psychic. For now, it's only important that you become familiar with your runes and the deeper meanings behind the stones. Read closely and learn them well.

Sun

One goal perfectly imagined is one goal
eventually achieved.

The healing and abundant light of the sun is essential. Without
it, our world would be left in shadows—we could neither thrive nor
see. In the past, most people had similar ideas and beliefs about the
sun. They associated the sun's nourishing rays with strength, fertility, creativity, and healing.

The Gypsy people called this sun glyph *cham*, and they used it
as a talisman against misfortune and evil. Because the sun is the
brightest star in the sky—the bringer of earthly light—it is symbolic of chasing ignorance out of the shadows while allowing truth
to take hold and grow.

Even now, in late summer the Plains Indians appeal to the
healing energies of the sun to bestow blessings during their *Wi
Wanyang Wacipi*, or Sun Dance. The ancient Egyptians associated the sun with divine guidance and called their Pharaohs
"sons of the Sun."

Drawing the Sun Stone during a reading implies a break in darkness, or a breakthrough. In fact, the appearance of the Sun Stone
can actually overpower any negative stones drawn, and should be
read accordingly.

The sun also represents radiance and magnetism, and the ability to draw to you what you need. The Sun Rune gives the power to overcome obstacles through self-mastery, discipline, and the projection of ego energies. The Sun can indicate sudden wealth, fame, or prestige. It stands for unlimited resources or the power to get things done.

Selecting the Sun Stone suggests you will soon be embracing the new and foretells of the falling away of the old or careworn from your life. You can look forward to a newfound enthusiasm, the combining of various energies to achieve a central goal, and an optimism that makes it possible to realize your dreams. This rune can also mean you will soon be free of limitations, you will escape misery, you will somehow become awakened, or that something previously hidden from you will be brought out into the light.

With another chapter beginning, a new set of tasks must be mastered. Therefore, the creation of a new role or persona to meet the expectations and challenges of your new life is very likely. Art, playfulness, and various forms of creative expression will somehow become a rewarding focus.

Since the sun's energy is usually thought to be masculine, drawing this stone can indicate a male authority figure assuming an important role in your success. However, the sun is just as likely to represent a female with a commanding vitality, vivaciousness, and strength. The Sun Rune can stand for the father, a husband, or a male relative in a reading as well. Another feature of sun energy foretells an ability to inspire the masses, to assume a role of leadership, or to be the center of attention in some capacity. Possibly at this time, you will be less tolerant of staying in the background and you will begin to want to see your efforts and hard work rewarded in a major way. If nothing else, the Sun Stone stands for that one big goal, and not the more trivial interests and affairs of your life.

But on a more mundane level, the Sun Stone can suggest a place where many people gather, risky business, a place of fun and levity, or a short-term love affair. The sun can even represent sexual overtures that are either surprising or unwanted. The sun is also the motivation behind plans being made. Whenever the sun is drawn, there is always something big in the works.

Also attributed to drawing the Sun Stone are curative powers, a period of healing or making life anew. Things put into action suddenly begin to culminate and yield positive results. This can even involve the gaining of status or a "star at its zenith." Now is a time of strength and clarity. In short, make the best of the situation because at the present time luck is very much on your side. Also expect important people to toss your name around. The forces acting behind your question are aligned favorably.

What happens is up to you—the individual. Overall, the Sun Stone foretells of people of high status making an appearance in your life. It can indicate the appearance of a teacher or guide. It is a representation of what is good, healthy, and right in your life. The Sun indicates love with a high energy, boundless joy, emotional and professional support.

Get ready for a turnaround when attention or recognition focuses in your direction. Likewise, you can expect grand results that grow and multiply into even greater things. The Sun Rune really means that you are now at the center of your own orbit. People cannot help but respond to the ideas and plans you've put into action.

At this time, you will want to especially beware of extravagance and lavish indulgences. You will also want to avoid making decisions based upon any kind of personal vanity or pride. The most effective route to success is to remain strong, sure, and confident while you proceed with both dignity and integrity. Now is the time that some of your most genuine efforts will be recognized.

Sun Rune in summary   Always a good omen, the Sun Rune means something of value is coming your way. You can look forward to taking a bold step or embarking on a new direction. Some may be carried out of their daily grind by unexpected and fortunate events.

Others will be made aware of added responsibility and will have to deal with it. The Sun Rune represents a place where money is exchanged; it represents material wealth and in some instances, *real riches*. This stone implies an important person with a title, a grand opening, or a much talked about event.

Expect public promotions and public affairs. Look to be amazed, dazzled, or even shocked by scandals. The Sun Rune stands for gaining a reputation or making your mark in a bigger way than you ever have before. Crowds, conventions, stages, or arenas may have something to do with the question you are now posing. An authority figure old enough to be a parent could have the right information or advice that you need right now. Look forward to status gained after the achievement of noteworthy goals. Accept your position as a mover and shaker in the world. For some of you, the time is right to head for the spotlight. For others, it's finally time to go for the gold.

Moon

Proceed from the dream outward . . .

Anaïs Nin

Always, the moon represents nocturnal awareness, that deep knowing found within the psyche and its layers of consciousness. When the sun hides away at the close of day, the moon becomes the brightest source of light in the sleeping world. No heavenly body has inspired as much poetry as the moon. In most cultures, the moon stands for the soulful imagination, inspired visions, and the richness that can surface out of darkness and dreams.

The Gypsies called the moon *shion,* or the "arms of protection," and this symbol was found on Gypsy talismans and drums. Early goddesses, such as Isis and Ishtar, wore the crescent crown, or horns of the moon. Since menstruation, or "the wise blood," has the same cycle as the moon (coming and going approximately every twenty-eight days), feminine powers are usually associated with the moon.

Because the moon bides her time and shows a different face each night, her powers have been underestimated. The moon has a subtle power, but with lasting effects. The Moon can also represent a change in emotional tone, as well as changes in general. When drawing this stone, you can expect a shift in focus or mood. This change will probably have an elusive echo effect, sending out waves and currents into every area of your life. This realization may be subtle at present, but the ramifications for change are powerful in the long run.

You could even say that your subject in question is going through a phase and changes will certainly come about but over a sustained period of time—that is, as long as you or your subject is willing to overcome habits and break negative patterns. Now is a good time to look at those patterns, and also defeat them, with an objective eye. It's likely the problem you are now confronting has origins in those you've brushed aside in the past. While you may feel this time is different, if you look at your dilemma more deeply, you may notice it involves many of the same old issues.

A more insidious meaning behind choosing this stone involves self-sabotage. Drawing the Moon Rune can mean that you are allowing life to happen to you, rather than making things happen. Sometimes this involves mindless passivity or making weak, half-hearted efforts because the road up ahead simply looks too hard and it's easier to allow your consciousness to go to sleep. The problem with this is, when you finally wake up, you may find that your efforts are too little, too late.

Since the Moon rules memory, it is difficult to let go of the past because the past makes up the very foundation upon which you now stand. You've made progress, but you've made mistakes, too. Therefore, it's best not to add more weight to a potential faultline in your foundation. Simply put, you won't be able to go along with the old way of doing things. Old habits and solutions you've relied on in the past just won't work anymore. In fact, they probably never did, and this is why you seem to be confronting the same issues over and over again.

The Moon Stone also speaks of the home, ancestors, female relatives, and the space you inhabit. The moon is where you feel the most insecure; it governs events from your childhood, both troubling or comforting, that you cannot seem to shake. Since the moon is associated with our deepest, most psychic needs, she can sometimes represent addictions, co-dependency, and the refusal to change. The moon wants comfort and reassurance. Since change means death to the old ways of doing things—and also the familiar—death is actually what the moon fears. When the Moon Stone turns up in a reading, the nucleus of your particular dilemma or question goes back in time and is somehow rooted in your childhood.

The Moon Stone suggests the feeling of being "moonstruck," acting impulsively, or being taken out of your better senses or right mind. This can represent a downfall, or an awakening, and sometimes both. It may even mean you are acting a bit loony or being totally impractical. The Moon Rune represents items of a domestic nature, things made of silver, mirrors, eyeglasses or contact lenses, love gifts given within the family (the extended family, as well), especially those involving weddings, anniversaries, births, and other milestone events.

In the past, the moon has been associated with sorcery, magick, and witchcraft—meaning you now have the ability to make a positive change through sheer determination and will—as long as your focus is strong and you do not waver.

Used positively, the moon suggests a birth, a new cycle, another beginning. It can indicate an eclipse in consciousness, a change in mind, or some wonderstruck epiphany. In some instances, the Moon Stone foretells a pregnancy or an expansion in your family or home. Perhaps this means you will be buying a house or building on to the one you already have. Perhaps it means you will need to isolate yourself in your own home to complete certain projects; or you may find that more of your daily work can now be done at home.

The moon's role in astrology is one which governs the imagination and creative expression. You may find your dreams are richer than usual; so much so, that you will be able to use this knowledge to the fullest benefit in your waking life. Often, when this stone is drawn, a powerful woman is about to enter your life who will give you the direction that you need. In fact, all associations with women will be beneficial at present, particularly if the other stones drawn are not especially negative. The Moon Rune implies delving into *the depths*. This can include finding safety and protection or finding your niche. It can mean facing old hurts or wounds of your past, especially those from your childhood or earliest memories. The Moon Rune also indicates creative talent, mother love, the pouring out from the depths of the soul, and connections with female energies.

Moon Rune in summary Relying on old ways of doing things could impede your success if you do not handle the moon's intuitive energy properly. Drawing the Moon Stone suggests wisdom gained through experience of memory, but it does not mean you should stay in a rut or stick to the kinds of bad habits that only forfeit your success. The idea of family, home, and ancestors is important now. Such memories may well be the key you need to unlock a certain puzzle that has been troubling you. This could imply a family secret—something that has not been properly explored or brought out into the open from your past. Drawing the Moon Stone says there will be a sudden shift in the circumstances that surround your immediate question. Bide your time before initiating any kind of action. This stone encourages calm and discourages haste. Think of this stone as a mirror where you receive the best results through patient reflection. You may need to ask a female who has connections to your past to get your answer. At any rate, now is the time to sleep lightly and pay attention to your dreams.

Flight

I have never really lived in the body anyway.
I have always lived beyond it, like a bird
flying beyond itself, but never really catching up
with where the mind takes it.

When we look at birds in flight, our souls cannot help but feel elevated, suddenly willing to break free from our limitations and boundaries. When we imagine flight, it's as if we move beyond ourselves, becoming one consciousness, one mind. *It is flight by which the mind and spirit soar.* Just recently, some scientists who study the brain have suggested that not only can the brain affect particles inside the body, it can also affect objects at a distance. It appears the mind does shape reality after all!

In Vahalla, the spirit world of the Teutonic peoples, it is said that Odin (All-Father), when not feasting with fallen warriors, liked to view the happenings of heaven and earth while sitting on his golden throne. When it was not possible for Odin to venture out of Vahalla, he sent his two ravens, *Hugin* and *Munin,* to fly over the world gathering information and news.

The idea of birds as messengers leaving the spirit world for the world of matter, and then returning with important news, is a universal theme. The Thunderbirds of Native American Plains tribes became messengers who brought a change in weather, and thus a change in insight and perspective by cracking open the sky and allowing spiritual visions to pour through as a refreshing rain.

Birds, in ancient lore, did not always have uplifting meanings. Even today, many believe that a bird flying inside the home, becoming trapped, or crashing against a window, is an omen of an impending death or dreadful news. Universally, birds indicate *spirit* on some fundamental level. They represent *transition*.

When the Flight Rune is selected, you can be certain transforming news is on its way. This piece of news is important because it will probably alter the direction you have already taken. It will give you hope, or it may force you to form a new strategy.

The outcome concerning the question you're now posing has already been put into action and the proper wheels are turning. Most likely, a decision has already been made. In any event, you will soon hear word concerning those matters which have occupied your mind recently. You will get your answer.

Be prepared for key communications to arrive from faraway places. Look for information with a twist, an unexpected announcement. Receiving messages through mental telepathy or by linking up on a mind-soul level is just another manifestation of the Flight Rune turning up.

This rune is mostly beneficial, and it would take an especially bad selection of stones to give your reading an overall negative effect. Instead, the Flight Rune often stands for glad tidings, essential information where you gain insight and knowledge, or communications that benefit the outcome of your question. This stone also indicates educated persons, a teacher, or a scholar.

The Flight Rune suggests messages of all kinds. Therefore letters, documents, business papers, and other forms of writing are pertinent to the question you have posed. Statements will be made, plans discussed; this matter will be talked over a great deal. At this time, you will probably need to rely on vehicles of communication involving the air: fax machines, phones, computer hookups, telegrams, and air mail. You may even take a sudden trip or become more involved with electronic media. It's likely that gadgets will become a more integral part of the work you do, and you will have to master new skills. Some of you can expect to bothered by ringing phones, machine noises, silly rumors, or busy chatter. Experiences of poltergeists, telepathy, and telekinesis are possible at this time. Expect very unusual happenings that cannot be explained by the usual logic or reasoning.

Spiritual activities of all types should surface, so it's best to approach them with a curious, but respectful state of mind. If so, there is probably no reason to be frightened of these consciousness-altering events. Look upon them as signs of divine wit, possibly angelic in nature.

More than any other, the Flight Rune represents winged thought and intuitive connections, so this rune is helpful to artists. Talent in the arts, especially music, dance, writing and painting rely upon the soaring thought of this creative energy. It brings to the forefront genuine intellect, leaping thought, divine inspiration, and using the mind in its highest capacity. When drawing this stone, the pace quickens. You can expect a speeding up of mental activity that can lead to unusual flights of genius, but also excessive nervousness and even insomnia, since the Flight Rune can represent being deprived of sleep.

Even more positively, you will begin to feel emancipated from the dregs of your past. There will be a lifting of obstacles, meaning increased opportunity, eventual freedom. Through knowledge and the right information, you take the higher road, and accomplish what you desire rather than bumping up against the usual blocks. No matter how chained or bound you are to an idea, a worry, bad credit, bad luck, or even a person who is bad for you, you can now "fly over it." You will be free.

Sometimes, when this rune is drawn, it can imply an uninvited guest coming to your home. It can represent meeting up with people who talk too much, someone who gossips without a conscience, or those who indulge in empty chatter just to keep the air moving. This stone can stand for wrong or misguided information that causes you to chase after false leads only to be left empty-handed or holding the bag.

In short, now is the time to take flight, to accept challenges without fear, to embrace change, to speak openly, to write what you know, to face that awe-inspiring risk while racing after sunlight and outdistancing clouds.

Choosing the Flight Rune speaks of a time when your mind is versatile and your reactions facile. You will be able to confront challenges and make the appropriate changes without the usual self-sabotaging emotionalism that figures in many human decisions. Some will become attuned to inborn psychic abilities. Others will rise above the rest while taking things lightly.

Flight Rune in summary   The Flight Rune stands for a time when you will overcome limitations and finally break free from the obstacles that have impeded your progress. You can look forward to a time when all communications are greatly important, including that of the unconscious mind, spiritual contacts, communications between this world and another, as well as more ordinary forms of communication, such as telephones, fax machines, and the mail. Expect to be given news that will alter your direction. Look to gain sudden insights and crucial revelations. Other meanings behind this rune are air travel, a visit to the airport, special deliveries, e-mail, computer communications, and phone calls. This rune signifies the kind of communication that changes your course of action, so there may be shake-ups or surprises in events you had already planned. Other meanings include the brain, mental explorations, or therapy. Flight also implies angelic guidance, special counsel, discussing future plans, and legal documents that may require your signature.

Rings

When you are beside me,
I feel that my self
has returned to myself.

Whenever two worlds meet, a different but related world is born out of the union that maintains the components of the two original worlds. As a child is born in a marriage, any type of bond or pledge between two individuals will also give birth to something new—hence, we have the Rings Rune.

In essence, the Rings Rune stands for an engagement, an agreement, a marriage, and sometimes an everlasting tie between two people. The two rings represent the wedding bands of the lovers. The third ring that holds them together stands for the bond that joins the lovers through eternity.

The Rings Rune always indicates joint efforts—some that are romantic in nature, others that are not. Simply put, the Rings Rune implies mutual support and a united front. Marriage and engagement are the simple explanations behind this stone, but it stands for much more. The Rings Rune actually indicates a pledge, or the binding of energies toward one dream, one goal to benefit both. It suggests the linking up of two (or more) souls who have agreed to work toward one purpose.

Throughout remembered history, rings have been thought to hold magickal properties. In this respect, the Rings Rune can indicate a stamp of approval, a blessing. It also represents the circle of protection that is found only in love, friendship, and mutual trust. These unions seem to be ordained by a higher power or authority. Therefore, the Rings Rune can represent the group mind or the collective soul.

When the Rings Rune is drawn, you can expect the appearance of a like-minded individual, a companion, someone to love, a sharing of sorts, or even a person you can compete with in a good-natured way. In some instances, drawing the Rings Rune can imply that a soul mate or a karmic companion is about to enter your life. Keep in mind, this does not always indicate a love affair or a romance. In any event, you will probably feel bound or connected to this person in some deep way.

The Rings Rune is related to beauty, and what it is you hold dear. At the same time, this ideal may somehow be unattainable—lost in dancing shadows and gorgeous mists. Perhaps the fulfillment of your dream is only slightly beyond your grasp. If not fulfilled, these ideals can transform into cravings for possessions, relationships, eros—anything to take your attention away from what it is you seem to lack. Perhaps the lack is spiritual or emotional. Therefore, the Rings Rune can represent the frustration found in aiming toward an ideal or goal that was never really meant to be yours.

The Rings Rune can also bring on the gaining of possessions, materialistic aims, and lavish pursuits. Dealings in art, cosmetics, perfumes, oils, literature, music, and fashion may somehow figure in your life very shortly. Buying or building a dream home and setting down roots are other likely scenarios. The Rings Rune is only materialistic in the sense that it symbolizes the building of a heaven on earth and the turning of ethereal dreams into material realities.

Rarely, drawing this stone can suggest an open battle or debate, but not with the usual treachery. It is a time when you will feel challenged by others, where you will be compelled to clarify your

interests and intentions. Concerns of a legal nature may even command your attention. Yet the Rings Rune is mostly fortunate, and
you will be able to draw upon your ability to charm others, to hold
their attention, and to eventually get what you're after through
noble or lofty actions.

Rings themselves were once believed to be tools of bewitchment,
able to hold others in bondage or to keep them under our spell.
Later, this symbol of "bondage" took on a more pleasant aspect as
it developed into a token of love and marriage. The appearance of
the Rings Rune in a reading can indicate you are bound to someone you can't get away from even though it may be best if you did.
It can mean responsibility to another person, a cause, a job, an
affair you can't walk away from.

   In this way, the Rings Rune becomes shiny handcuffs rather than
golden wedding bands—rings that are so tight and binding even a
Houdini cannot slip out of them! Perhaps you do not want to be
let go at this point. Perhaps there is still something important that
needs to be worked out before moving on to the next level, another
series of experiences. At any rate, in some circumstances the rings
can symbolize shackles of bondage.

   Whatever your reason, if this particular meaning rings true for
you, now may be the time to reevaluate many of your key relationships. It may be a time when you will simply have to go it alone,
unable to depend on those who've rallied to your aid in the past.
Never fear. This stone also predicts the meeting up with certain
individuals who can help advance your cause, your goals, your
ideals, and your dreams.

   On a more mundane level, the Rings Rune is a rather neutral
stone, somewhat benign and lacking in the kind of energy it takes
to bring on strong action and change. If your question or subject is
pressing, the appearance of the Rings Rune is not always a good
omen, as it can indicate airy smiles, empty handshakes, and agree-
able people though no real progress is being made. In some

instances, you won't get a straight answer, as those involved will pass the buck, and few will be concerned about the urgency of your matter.

The Rings Rune not only implies intimacy, as is found in a marriage or romance, but it also speaks of how we connect with others socially.

Rings Rune in summary The Rings Rune always implies important alliances and agreements. Drawing this rune can suggest "hatching a plan" or aligning your energies with another toward the successful completion of your goals. When this rune turns up, it can indicate dealings with intimate associates, such as a spouse or a lover, or the meeting up with a soul mate. The Rings Rune symbolizes all bonds including marriage, the wedding day, a celebration, happy couplings, and joint interests. This particular rune also indicates cliques, groups, and social affairs.

You can look for an important gathering very soon, such as an engagement, court proceedings, the signing of documents or papers alongside another person, and sometimes the dissolution of joint ventures, or facing enemies straight on. Coupled with the Scythe Rune, turning up the Rings can mean a divorce or separation, the parting of old friends, or a feud.

More routinely, selecting the Rings Rune will suggest being charmed by the superficial, going through the motions, beautiful surfaces that yield nothing of importance, gentility, popular culture, members of the wedding, attractive individuals, status seekers, sudden popularity, group support, and even a laughing or applauding crowd.

Romance

This love is a sword placed between us . . .

The Romance Rune brings on the smoky light and slow burn of attraction and erotic love. A stone of extremes, it represents magnetism on many levels. Pictish (old Scottish) in origin, the Romance Rune signifies the essence of life and survival instincts. There's little doubt this symbol was meant to stand for the creative potential and spiritual connotations expressed in sexual love. In an upright position, the rune suggests the male sexual organs just before the act of creation. Turned in the opposite direction, the Romance stone seems to suggest the womb and ovaries of the female in a state of receptivity.

Something begins here, where there is a charge, a leap, a conception. Here, desire is a divine power not meant to be overcome. *It should be embraced.* In essence, this rune stands for sharing what you have, the ultimate give and take.

The Romance Rune also symbolizes the leaping dance of creation. The fundamental meaning behind the rune is "to spark"—a term still used by hill people in Appalachia, and also in the south— meaning to initiate a relationship or to start a new phase. Thus, sex is only one meaning behind this complex rune.

The three-petaled glyph, representing the Holy Trinity, is still found in many Christian churches, but this symbol and idea traces back as far as the Ancient Egyptians, suggesting the three-chambered heart and its corresponding intelligences. The Egyptians called the heart intelligence *Ab*, which represented life and desire radiating outward. In connection with this, were minor intelligences falling under the rulership of the *Ab* and they were: the *mer* intelligence, meaning to bind, combine and merge; the *usehk* intelligence representing separation of the soul from the body, estrangement and feeling the phantom loss of otherness. In this way, the Egyptians showed us that the heart not only rules the passions, it holds the highest forms of intelligence, ones based upon our instincts, the life force that exists within the heart.

Drawing this stone has multiple meanings. Obviously, it can indicate romantic interests that are present or coming into your life shortly. However, the romance or affair in question could be an illusion that promises much but actually delivers little in any permanent kind of way.

For the less starry-eyed and the already happily in love, the Romance stone has more practical implications. Some can expect becoming involved in a triangle, where you act as go-between. There may even be sneaky, clandestine events surrounding friends and coworkers, such as illicit affairs, undercover work, or scandals. (Take your pick.)

The Romance Rune also turns up when there is a surge of power behind the meaning of the question that has been posed. In short, if the Romance Rune could speak, it would say, "Your inquiry has deep and foreboding implications. Put away childish needs and demands. Things are serious now."

Sometimes we associate hidden powers with something that is evil or ominous, but when the Romance Rune is selected in a reading it is usually a good omen. This stone lends strength and passion to works-in-progress and projects just beginning.

We can't ignore one fundamental meaning behind this stone and that is to fascinate, to infatuate, to hold sway over, to bewitch, or to fall under a spell. In keeping with this, the Egyptians believed the strength of the heart, or *Ab,* was behind all successful magic so this rune is very important when it comes to spell-casting and all forms of sympathetic magic.

When drawing this stone, you can look forward to a sudden turn of events that sets you on a different path. Watch out for a sweeping away of the old, and perhaps even a crisis or a scare that brings new angles to old ways of doing things and perhaps a startling revelation.

Since the Romance Rune stands for transforming passions, you can expect a complete lack of objectivity over the question you are now posing. It goes without saying this is something you feel deeply about. However, you must realize that we often drive away the things we care the most about by the tunnel vision of our desires. Having focus may not be all it is cracked up to be. Writers and artists can tell you that the more they fixate on their craft, the more likely they are to drive away the inspiration that prompts their creative visions. You should be very careful about what you wish for. You may certainly receive this wish, but in a way you never expected or were not prepared for.

In any event, look for instant attractions, relationships of unusual complexity, or a strong soul connection. Also look for a temptation, some intrigue, or a breaking scandal. Be prepared for events that seem fated and read the signs accordingly. Expect dramatic happenings or being swept away by your passions.

Sometimes this rune presents itself in readings where there is a craving for power, or a craving to be "filled." Although there is beauty here, you will also find a neediness that cripples the initial passion or desire. Therefore, instead of some creative flowering, you may find a soul withering. There may even be a wish to be consumed by desire, where the ego is totally obliterated. Likewise, you may feel a need to merge or form some greater alliance with another person or ideal. But beware of dangerous temptations or developments that compel you to go against your better sense.

Now is the time to take that bold step and embrace a new direction that is somehow related to your innermost passions. All life-transforming events begin with a risk. Just make sure you step back in time, so you may be dazzled by the fireworks but not get burned.

Romance Rune in summary   The Romance Rune suggests a great desire surfacing in your life, becoming infatuated with a person different from the people you normally associate with. Turning up this stone indicates being drawn into situations or affairs that defy reason, witnessing an illicit act, instant attractions, or being swept away by forces outside of your control.

This stone carries with it forces that drive us beyond our usual good sense, sometimes indicating charismatic, controversial individuals with hidden or secret motives. There will be good luck in the short term as the Romance Rune denotes excitement and getting fired up by daring new plans and options. It can also indicate being obsessed with an idea or a person, and feeling that you must somehow follow through no matter what the cost. This rune suggests there is great energy behind the matter you are posing and you can use it in a positive way. But the energies behind this stone can also be used to tear down and destroy, so be forewarned.

On a mundane level, the Romance Rune stands for the reproductive organs, bodily fluids, good sex, a fantasy which is not easily shared because of certain taboos, and sometimes sexual or romantic addictions. It indicates an extremely powerful bond between two people that is not necessarily sexual. Sometimes the Romance Rune represents a mentor-student relationship. Turning up this stone can suggest a love affair where the lovers are of vastly different ages or backgrounds. Regardless of your question, you can be assured there is great power behind the matter you are posing, and the power can be used for good, as well as bad, so be aware of your choices and the consequences they may bring.

Woman

... moon in Cancer, she said.
Tonight, that chilled orchid with her neon glow,
(meaning) the woman is dreaming again.

The Woman Rune signifies a vital, shining power and gentle action. The appearance of this stone in any reading brings on safety, protection, and a soft cosmic nudge. Of course, not all females are soft or yielding. However, the real message behind the Woman Rune is one that shows us that by offering our compassion and care for others, we are not losing power, we are actually gaining strength. In essence, this rune implies female power—sure and strong—the kind that nurtures and creates.

Part of this rune is the womanly V that harks back to the ancient Egyptians' Doorway of Isis, which they believed led us into *the infinite*. According to the Egyptians, this is the doorway through which all life is called into being. It can also be a doorway of departure by which we leave this world.

The branching V, representing a woman or a girl, is a universal idea. This particular symbol corresponds to the Finnish rune for *Ilmater*, meaning "water mother"; it also stood for the Virgin Mother among Germanic peoples during the Middle Ages. Other groups associated this symbol with the magic wand.

With some ties to the earlier crescent moon, the Woman Rune suggests the wisdom of the heavenly bodies and starry nights. It is through this fertile darkness that all mysteries are revealed. It is also the moist womb in which buried ideas and feelings are submerged, locked away like forbidden treasure.

The branching V of the Woman Rune stands for the lineage of the tribe or the branches of the family tree. It suggests tracing back to the extended family, generations, and the heritage of the womb rather than moving forward to gain knowledge and power. It can also represent the branching of the creative imagination and speculation or becoming centered and then flowering outward. Likewise, her branches symbolize the dexterity of the fingers that can tie up loose ends and stitch together the details. This stone stands for the female line, friendships, and friendly alliances. Its symbol denotes a circle of protection.

Obviously, when the Woman Rune symbol turns up, a woman is the concern or has influence over the question you are posing. Sometimes it turns out that it is a female who intervenes, or acts as a go-between, clearing up misunderstandings or blocks. Perhaps, it is you who work as the go-between or are somehow the key decision maker.

Usually this rune works as an agent for good, but in some instances it can imply meddling or even a type of motherly smothering. It can bring on a period of time when you must break free from the binds of love, especially those associated with your childhood, immediate family, or early life.

One manifestation of this rune selection is a love affair, usually one that is based upon pleasantries and mutual interests. Another is the presence or appearance of an attractive person; one who is also popular and admired, one who is able to win friends and friendly alliances.

Coupled with the Moon Rune, the Harvest Rune, or Romance Rune, the Woman Rune can foreshadow an impending pregnancy or a love affair that is blossoming into one that is more stable or at least happier.

This brings up a another element of the Woman Rune: its associations with midwifery and obstetrics. After all, this stone encompasses everything that is female in nature, and giving birth is certainly important in many women's lives. Therefore, when this symbol turns up, fertility issues, or those involving the functions of sexuality, may have something-to do with the question that has been posed. This stone can also represent a woman who leads a group or a cause, or a person who holds dominion over the home, hearth, or the domestic arts.

One of the higher manifestations of this symbol is its ability not only to heal, but also to point out healing ability in various guises. Certainly, this rune indicates herbal and alternative medicines. It may also involve a healing of the psyche where the soul is at the center and is the core of our totality as persons.

Although the Woman Rune stands for feminine power and energy, healers are not always women. Men too can be nurturers and healers. But healers, regardless of gender, still tap into the nourishing type of energy the Woman Rune suggests. Often a healer is the healer of friends, the healer of the neighborhood, or even the healer of the community. Healers can use words to heal. They can use touch. They can use their inborn psychic powers and abilities. In this way, the Woman Rune indicates an energy present in your life which promises to soothe and make right whatever is wounded or unresolved.

Turning up the Woman Rune is generally favorable when doing a reading involving romance. However, there is a gentle action behind this stone. Often the romance is necessary for growth and healing, but it may not be a long-term one that leads to marriage or a commitment. What is necessary when drawing this stone is learning to appreciate the gifts of cooperation.

In essence, do not expect fast actions regarding the matter of your concern. It's likely the situation has not yet been resolved. You may need to put forth another strong effort in order to achieve what you desire. However, you can expect to find others receptive to your plans and also a fair judgment concerning this issue.

Woman Rune in summary   To select the Woman Rune foretells a
period of healing and rejuvenation. It can suggest finding a place or
a niche where you can be yourself, where all things flourish and
grow. The Woman Rune suggests love and nourishment but in a
natural way where we abide by the rules and cycles of nature, where
we are not governed so much by personal needs.

This rune stands for women, the woman in question, and can
also suggest the possibility of a pregnancy or the growth and
beginning of a new project or achievement. Other meanings signify purity, harmony, peace, beauty, and balance. When this rune
is drawn you can expect gentle action rather than shattering
changes. Look for the wisdom of mothers, daughters, grandmoth-
ers, aunts, and sisters. The Woman Rune also stands for the witch's
magick wand, the healer, psychic, and woman of mysterious ways.
When picking this rune, you can expect receiving something of
value of a sentimental nature, stability in your life, comfort, or a
"take-charge" individual. Look for growth, fertility, a garden, land
inherited, or the family home being somehow important in the
question you are posing.

The Woman Rune symbolizes a dwelling place, your life's path in
accordance with the powers of nature, the path you take, a time for
healing, impartiality, fairness, and judgment. This stone's turning
up implies embracing the new and untried with a nurturing center
of support to fall back on as well as embracing what is beautiful
and good in life.

Man

Energy is eternal delight . . .

William Blake

The Man Rune is an extremely old symbol and you can find variations of it in all cultures. As the inversion of the womanly V, it's obvious the Man Rune represents the male member in an aroused state. But this aroused state is not always sexual. In fact, most of the time it is not. The real message behind the Man Rune is to take action, to proceed or go forward as planned and also to confront.

This symbol has been the Germanic sign for victory; it stands for the raised sword in battle. As an arrow on its side, the Man Rune corresponds to the Anglo-Saxon *Kaen*, which means to "open" or to find a way. Nordic peoples called this sign *Tac*, which represented the facing down of an enemy or a foe. In any event, the bottom line to this rune implies defensive action, a speeding up of activity or confrontation.

In a reading, choosing this rune rarely suggests violence or fighting, but it can mean you will need to defend your own interests. You will have to stand strong. This is not a good time to move slowly, go inward, or reflect. Conversely, you will need to move quickly concerning your question.

Turning up the Man Rune adds dynamics and power to any reading. This stone indicates vitality, willpower, the drive and necessary energy to get things done. Often the forces behind this stone are disruptive, unexpected, representing upheaval and drastic change. But this is not necessarily bad. In daily living, there should always be balance. A life without change or action can be intolerable even to the gentlest of souls. After all, action is energy and energy is life.

In a short while, you can expect to be challenged heartily, and you can expect to have the resources to meet this challenge. This is not a positive time to coast or allow things to happen on their own. You must be the one who makes an effort or gives the first shove. Without discipline, this energy suggests all hell could break loose. Without foresight and strength of purpose, certain events in your life could go awry. You must also be willing to defend many of your beliefs, your integrity, and your opinions. Unless otherwise suggested in the reading, backing down is probably not the best move for you to make at the present time.

On a mundane level, the Man Rune implies a male, most often an important male figure in your life. However, you can also read this stone as an amazing person with a wellspring of energy and resources, because this symbol can stand for individuals who are dynamic, with lots of nervous energy, for movers and shakers, and for people who are physically active or even confrontational. Drawing this stone can sometimes imply a troublemaker who wishes to sabotage you or usurp any authority you might have.

Of course, there is the possibility of unnerving clashes with the opposition and irritating circumstances that frustrate you or block your efforts. What this rune is saying is that you will not be able to accomplish what you have in mind, or get your wish, with any sense of calm or ease at present. In fact, you may have a fight on your hands. Therefore, you can expect challenges that will be overt, in an in-your-face kind of way. These conflicting circumstances will be impossible to ignore. Several scenarios might take place. For instance, someone may single you out to overpower or defeat you. You will begin to feel deeply irritated or squelched at this time. Some will have to deal with unexplained feelings of hostility. If you're not much of a fighter, this situation could prove to be quite stressful and nerve-wracking. It's a good time to polish up on some of your defensive skills. Likewise, a person may single you out to mock, destroy or ridicule publicly. But you must hold your ground until some change breaks the tension, freeing you up for new action.

The secret to handling this kind of aggressive energy is that it peters out pretty quickly. Here is the rule of thumb: Bullies are essentially cowards. Confidence and surety of purpose unnerves them, so now is the time to face them head-on. Sometimes bullies are thrust in to our lives just so we can find out how strong and competent we really are. It is fundamentally important that you meet this challenge now. If you do withdraw, you can be certain this scenario will continue to present itself until you have mastered what it is you need to learn.

You may also want to beware of the possibility of someone sabotaging your efforts in a sneaky, covert way, sometimes by simply undermining your confidence. Usually this is the kind of aggression and hostility we tend to encounter from "friends," or people who know us on some intimate basis. Most likely this hostility is covered up, and you may find it difficult to pinpoint precisely why things seem to be going wrong. You may notice you tend to lose confidence around certain friends or family members; pay attention to this. It is most important that you defend your decisions and not be swayed or controlled by situations your better sense tells you to ignore.

On a more benign note, usually when the Man Rune turns up in a reading, you can expect the outcome of your question to progress much faster than you expected. The Man Rune holds a speedy, impatient energy. In fact, you will most likely learn some important information that pertains to this question or reading within the next few days. Therefore, it's important to watch all of the signs concerning the matter of your question.

Man Rune in summary The Man Rune implies force. It can indicate a weapon, a blow, to strike or to hit, and other forms of opposition. It suggests linking up with individuals who are pushy, or those who apply more force than is necessary. This rune infers action and suggests that the matter you are posing will develop much more quickly than you had previously expected.

The Man Rune represents a boy or a man, a warrior, a soldier, a person in a uniform, the military, as well as law enforcement. This rune suggests timely action on a current matter. If you move promptly you can expect big benefits. If not, an opportunity may slide by.

This rune comes with a warning that certain forces in your life may have run amuck. It indicates shocking or surprising developments. It can suggest insults or verbal abuse. At this time you may feel a need to be emancipated from strife or restriction in your life. Be wary of impetuous actions.

On a mundane level, the Man Rune stands for heat and fevers, so when drawn this rune indicates illnesses, viruses, or infections. Not all bad, when this stone turns up it energizes all of the others and speeds things so you won't have to wait so long for your outcome. The Man Rune represents energy, zest, enthusiasm, ideals, and hopes. You can expect rapid changes and thrilling situations. So be prepared to take a bold step.

ḣαʀvest

The force that through the green fuse drives the flower
Drives my green age . . .

Dylan Thomas

The Harvest Rune depicts the abundance of wheat (or another essential grain) ready to be harvested. This rune signifies all kinds of fortune, good luck, and bounty, especially around career or material gain.

This early symbol is partly governed by Zeus, the Greek god of thunder, clouds, mountains, and weather—the preserver of life who reigns over the harvest and the fruitfulness of the fields. The Romans called their version of this god Jupiter (for which the great benefic planet is named). He is known for his vastness, lack of limitations, and generosity of spirit. But it's the energy of the goddess Juno (queen of the Gods and Jupiter's female counterpart) who holds the most sway over the Harvest Rune. Juno is often shown with flowing, flaxen hair, an ample figure, holding a gilded staff or wand and wearing a golden breastplate. Juno is a protectress who rewards diligence and hard work with what we now call a lucky break. Many of Juno's rewards are easy ones to appreciate since she is not as concerned with changing heavens and expansive skies as Jupiter is. Instead, Juno promises material gain.

Others read this rune as the straw that is cut to make the witch's broom, an earthy object that magically carries the witch across velvety black skies, across space and time and the obstacles that leave her earthbound. Even before the appearance of the witch's broom in old European lore, it was the Egyptian Isis who was said to sweep with an armload of wheat across the heavens, dropping bits of splendor to form the dazzling display of the Milky Way.

Turning up the Harvest Rune in a reading predicts rewards and benefits of the most excellent kind. Like the grain, the appearance of this stone brings into your life what is absolutely essential to your well-being, growth, and happiness. The result will depend entirely upon the individual asking the question: How much are you willing to invest? Some may seek spiritual growth while others seek financial riches or security. The blessings the Harvest Rune gives can only expand while nourishing body, soul, and spirit in this time of positive change.

When the Harvest Rune makes an appearance in a reading, it indicates that what you've worked so hard to achieve will finally bear fruit and probably in a bigger way than you expected. Look forward to a time of easy flow, optimism, and fortunate developments where you are able to encompass more and take the necessary risks to fulfill your desires. Think *abundance, increase,* and *fruitfulness* and go on from there. Whatever you begin now will only grow and flourish. Better yet, obstacles are now being lifted, paving the way toward many of your greatest hopes and dreams. A door opens, and you enter ready to meet challenges and embrace each change.

It has been said that the Goddess Juno gave Jupiter an immortal tree with golden fruit on their wedding day. As long as their love thrived, as legend has it, the tree would continue to bear fruit. The Harvest Rune foretells of blessings bestowed, but the secret behind this blessing relies entirely upon how much you are willing to work and generate positive energy in order to manifest these blessings. If you put forth only halfhearted efforts, you will still receive a blessing, but usually not anything that would make a substantial difference in your life. However, if you are willing to put forth a genuine effort, you can expect fortunate results and some even beyond your wildest dreams.

Turning up the Harvest Rune is a definite green light, but you would be wise to watch all of the signs in order to make your dream a reality. In other words, you must take responsibility for your good fortune and use these positive developments wisely. You would do well to avoid foolish risks, overspending, mindless thrill-seeking, and meaningless pleasures.

For spiritual seekers, drawing the Harvest Rune can predict the meeting of an important teacher, a sympathetic judge, or a helpful and discerning guide. You can expect to meet an individual with spiritual authority (although not necessarily a religious person) who will help you embark on a right course of action through humor or wisdom, or who will simply act as a catalyst or devil's advocate. Such a teacher will reveal herself or himself by expressing a full heart, boundless enthusiasm, spirit, and energy.

At this time, you will be able to overcome limitations that have previously restricted you. You can turn weaknesses into strengths, drawing the rewards, gifts, and accolades into the niche you have carved out for yourself. It is very important to have a clear vision right now, avoiding the confusion or muddled thinking that might have held you back in the past.

Although the Harvest Rune is extremely lucky whenever it turns up in a reading, certain stones, such as the Scythe or the Crossroads Runes, can cancel out some good fortune coming your way. However, it's important not to lose hope if this happens. Anytime this symbol presents itself happier days are ahead for you, and you are quite likely to get your wish. No matter what, good luck will find you, knocking down walls, opening doorways, and leading you down the right path to claim your prize.

Harvest Rune in summary   The most positive stone of all, the Harvest Rune indicates the spirit of protection and good fortune. You can expect doorways to open and all manner of benefits to surround your matter in question. Expect lucky developments, shining achievements, recognition, awards, and accolades. This is a time when doorways open and obstacles are lifted. Whenever the Harvest Rune turns up, you can expect an increase in all areas of your life, especially in the areas of money or love. Look for unexpected gifts, pleasant surprises, and situations which work out in your favor. The Harvest Rune stands for many things but it always represents gains, expansion, and easy flow as far as your goals are concerned.

Look for an opening which sets you on the right path, giving thanks and receiving thanks, the meeting up with or a reunion with your one true love, expansion as well as excess and exaggeration. Other benefits may have to do with buying and selling property, blazing a new path, carving a niche or corner in the market, as well as all manner of fortunate events.

Now is the time when many of your cherished dreams will finally be realized. Always a good omen, the Harvest Rune promises gains and fulfillment. Look for guidance from the wise and learned, and expect to hit your mark.

CROSSROADS

I go down to the Crossroads,
I try to flag a ride.
Don't nobody seem to know me.
Everybody just pass me by.
Sun goin' down,
Dark gonna catch me here!
Sun goin' down,
Dark gonna catch me here!

from *Crossroad Blues*, Robert Johnson

The Crossroads, also called Crossed Spears, was generally considered an evil omen by the Gypsy peoples as well as African Americans in the past. But when it appears in a reading, this stone is not all bad. This is especially true for those who embrace change or strive for solid achievement and for those willing to embark in a new direction.

Throughout the world, crossroads are thought to hold special powers related to the mysterious forces of the night. In eastern Europe, vampires were thought to lurk at crossroads, waiting to feed upon the next victim who happened to pass by. In Germany, to meet your *Doppelgänger*, or "body double" walking toward you at the crossroads surely meant your impending death. Hecate suppers were a tradition in southern Europe where cakes decorated with candles, and other luscious foods, were left as offerings at crossroads in order to win favor from Hecate, awesome Goddess of the underworld, mystery, and darkness. Universally, the symbol of the crossroads seems to have brought out feelings of anxiety and unease. In both Europe and the United States, murderers were often hanged at the crossroads to later confuse their ghosts. Likewise, there were stories of the Devil tempting weary souls at the crossroads, by testing their fortitude and their wills. In early America, suicides were buried at the crossroads so their unhappy spirits would finally be able to rest in peace; this was also thought to prevent their becoming earthbound phantoms.

When this stone is selected, you can expect opposition, either subtly or overtly. Many of your efforts will feel stopped or frozen, and it will be impossible for you to move forward until a new course of action is decided upon. Some of you may feel trapped, where all directions appear to be the wrong ones. It's even possible you will become intimately involved with people who do not support you—although this may be covered up. In keeping with this, it may seem like a lonely time when you face the world alone and the only strength you can draw upon is your own.

Some who pick this stone will experience the frustration of delays, causing them to repeat their efforts several times as a way of finally manifesting their goals. When your dream finally becomes a part of you, it is only then that the universe can respond to your wishes or desires. In Zen Buddhism, it is believed that we can only realize our dreams when we give up our attachments to them, when they contribute to a plan greater than ourselves. In this way, the Crossroads represents how we fall victim to desires which really have little to do with our happiness or spiritual growth.

It is now time to look at the big picture and allow such dreams to generate energy on their own. You might consider putting them aside for a while. Turning up the Crossroads can mean it's your turn to get in the trenches with the rest of humanity and pay your dues. This may not be exactly fun, but you must work hard and finish all plans and goals in order to achieve the kind of successes that you can enjoy later.

You may be tempted to abandon a plan that seems plagued by misfortune or bad timing. Usually when this stone is drawn it means you only need to change your approach and not your goal. This is not a time when things come easily or too soon; therefore, you will probably have to try and try again.

Whatever you set out to accomplish at this time will be met with resistance. Matters you've depended on may fall through, leaving you to face the situation alone. The crossroads reading of this stone implies that you may forced to recover what you can while accepting certain losses. Arguments or disagreements may arise since the Crossroads Rune stands for enemies. You can expect open confrontation, possibly a certain harshness or lack of sympathy from others where you will be challenged to defend what is yours.

This is also a time when everything slows down to a crawl. However, it's important to keep in mind that any effort you put forth at present will be lasting and enduring. In a short while, you will realize that the final results are more substantial than any win you may have scored rather easily. Not only that, you will see that you have gained the courage and wisdom to meet such challenges in the future.

In the meantime, your will is being tested and you will face certain frustrations that may seem to be more trouble than they are worth. Keep in mind that you are putting down the foundations for your future; you would not want to build the rest of your life on a faulty foundation.

Drawing the Crossroads Rune implies fated events that may appear out of your control; many of these fated events will seem rather harsh or negative at the time. It's best to consider the overall

picture. If you feel held back or squelched, it's important to realize that this is probably for a good reason. In the future, you may
thank your lucky stars that any impetuous actions have been
stopped in their tracks before bringing misfortune and mishap
into your life.

Standing at the crossroads is the Grandmother—or Grandfather—
spirit, the snow-haired wizened one who holds the silvery cup of
knowledge and discernment that you need. Of course, this figure is
not beautiful in any temporal way. Her eyes are covered by the
scum of blindness. Her weary spine is curved with age, and her
careworn face is etched with the ravages of time. Yet what she holds
is wisdom gained through trial and error, insight learned only
through hardship and mistakes. What the Grandmother spirit
offers is the gift of *sound judgment*, the gift of *truth* and *correction*.
There are four directions and the Grandmother spirit points her
bony finger one way. Which path should you take? The one that
leads ahead—not back—and into the future.

Crossroads Rune in summary   This rune indicates a more difficult
path where things are not so easy. The Crossroads represents not
only quarrels, misunderstandings, open enemies, and adversarial
relationships, but also discipline and mastery over the self. In this
way, the Crossroads is not necessarily bad luck, as its descriptions
might imply. It stands for slow, but substantial gains.

On a mundane level, the Crossroads Rune suggests maintaining
the status quo, understanding boundaries and limitations, making
a sustained effort, practical matters, and solid achievement. Relationships may be on shaky ground when one of these elements is
sacrificed at the expense of the other. On a more basic level, the
Crossroads stands for elders who are able to share their wisdom.

This rune stresses basic concerns, the bottom line, solitude, and
reassessing your losses. It can indicate feeling boxed in, separation,
being shut out by someone you love, or even jail. There may be

feelings of discouragement or dejection when the Crossroads Rune turns up.

However, this rune promises that you will soon discover innate strengths and resources. In this way what you finally achieve by hard work will have a deeper meaning than wins you gain from lucky breaks.

Star

When we count the burning stars,
these are the souls which cannot be extinguished.
They thrive on light, not air.
The soul is most beautiful without the body
when it cannot be counted
being here.

In ancient times, the star symbol was called the Star of Ishtar or Queen of Heaven by the Akkadians and Mesopotamians. She was the goddess of divinity, beauty, peace and also war. Later, the Gypsies reinterpreted this earlier glyph as the sign of the Magi who followed the lone, bright, unrelenting star to light their way in search of the Christ child.

The image of the star became a metaphor for the idea that there is really no one way to reach our star or destination, since we each attain it by following different paths. Astrologers still use this symbol to represent a sextile, or aspect of easy flow and luck in a birth chart. In the past, alchemists used this symbol to represent the planet Venus.

Other cultures also associated the star symbol with Venus, or morning star. But it was during the Middle Ages that the Knights of Templar (an esoteric organization predating the Freemasons in

Europe) stumbled upon the fact that when the movements of Venus were studied and mapped out from earth, its revolutions formed an exact pentacle, or six-pointed star.

Revolution is one meaning the Star Rune implies. Yet, the revolution of the Star Rune is a revolution with a focus, one with the glinting brightness of humane intelligence and conscious forethought. In this way the star becomes the realization of practical ideals, the hope of redemption, and the pursuit of long-range plans and dreams.

In the Tarot, the eight-pointed star signifies learning, accomplishment, and the power gained through what is placed before us, that which seems predestined or ordained by the heavens. What develops may appear to be a lucky break to others, but this is usually not the case since the Star Rune actually indicates achievement and advancement won through a long or sustained effort, especially those related to your ideals, your loftier beliefs, and higher impulses. In this way, the Star Rune reveals the sparkle and ease of wisdom and strength; this is not the wisdom suggested by the Crossroads Rune that is the wisdom gained through doing time and suffering. In short, your world is opening up and things are getting brighter. The star up ahead will lead you down the right path, giving you heart and a direction.

Basically, drawing the Star Rune in a reading is an affirmation, a sign that is greatly positive. This stone advises that it's time to move on and pursue your purest dreams or ideals. Sometimes this can mean that what you are now working on will go public, or will somehow be elevated or transformed into something larger than what you previously had in mind. More than anything else, the symbol of the star suggests that you should have faith in what you are now doing. The prizes won through the star are certainly not won easily, but they have a steadiness and a brightness that branch out into many areas of your life, not just the question you are now posing.

For some, this can mean aligning yourself and your energies with a cause that is greater than yourself. In this way, the Star Rune represents a unity found in ideals, moving toward some collective focus. After all, the star is what we yearn for. Thus, this tiny seed of light is actually an entire solar system holding the complexities of your future, even though you may not be able to see all of the details at present. You can expect to win gains through risk, faith, and speculation.

One of the more basic meanings behind the Star Rune involves money or finances. Usually this can indicate a windfall, a sudden fortunate event that changes or transforms the way you use money or an increase in your income for the better. The Gypsies associate the Star Rune with an engagement, a celebration, or a betrothal—usually involving the giving of a piece of jewelry, an heirloom, or some other precious item that signifies the pledging of oneself to another.

Among the runes, the Star Rune stands out by virtue of its sparkle, brightness, and luminosity. When the Star Rune appears in a reading, it suggests that in a short while you will be singled out for your own vision as an individual, or you may be asked to act as a spokesperson for an idea, a belief, or a purpose that represents many. In some instances the Star Rune can signify sudden fame or a promotion, a happening or an event that can bring on unpredictable upsets, unexpected publicity, or a swift change of action. Despite what develops you can look upon such changes as positive, fast-paced, and exciting.

"To thine own self be true" is one message behind the Star Rune, but this does not mean you should act only for yourself and your own interests at this time. To the contrary, by finding your direction, you will enable others with a fainter vision to discover their own course through the strides and efforts you have worked for and attained. This will mean taking the lead and breaking down old structures, making way for new ones. Now's the time to focus in, to go forward, and broaden your horizons regardless of risks. This may mean you will need to travel a long way, crossing over vast distances (both physical and emotional), to achieve the full measure of your dream. The real message behind the Star Rune is: *Your solution may be a revolution.* Stop holding still waiting for lightning to strike! Keep the faith and keep moving. Dreamers see what's up ahead.

Star Rune in summary   This rune indicates the realization of a dream or a wish that has been extremely meaningful to you. It suggests a ray of hope, a gem, a prize, divinity, and some crowning achievement. When picking this stone you can expect the crystallization of long-term dreams or plans, the presence of higher guides, spirituality, the meeting of angels or avatars, and the immediate future.

Drawing this rune promises several fortunate developments in your life. Look for an event which shatters all of your preconceived notions of what your life should be. Now is the time when something good can be salvaged from what has been lost or destroyed. Soon, many areas of your life will be completely transformed. Drawing this rune suggests certain events that may be stranger than fiction, the taking on of what has been untried or unproven, risks, leaps of faith, Now is a time when you will be dissatisfied with the mundane or the ordinary.

The Star Rune suggests all kinds of financial and material gains as well. You can expect money, possible wealth, assets, being in on a prosperous venture, becoming famous or renowned, precognition or prophetic visions, wishes granted, and a positive turn of events. Other meanings include heavenly favors, lightning storms, electricity, the sky, innovation, inspiration, and a crystal-clear direction. Look for gifts, such as a piece of jewelry, a bulletin or a news flash, wishes granted, the presence of higher guides, a godchild or an heir, understanding your purpose, and seeing waves of the future.

Waves

My soul is an enchanted boat,
which, like a sleeping swan, doth float,
upon the silver waves . . .

Percy Bysshe Shelley

Part of the Waves Rune—the spiral—is one of the oldest symbols. In many cultures it has stood for the coils of consciousness that spiral back to a divine source. Spirals have been discovered on bronze jewelry in the ice-capped lands of the northern peoples, beside the azure waters of Crete, imprinted on ancient pottery in the Near East, and even in the desert lands of the American Southwest. Universally, the spiral represents power and movement. The Gypsy peoples called this rune with spirals Waves, indicating forward motion, and they associated it with long journeys by which the traveler is somehow transformed or changed.

In astrology, water is the element of sacrifice and guilt. It is the element of sinners and saints, the element of mermaids and witches. It is also the element of creativity and the visionary imagination. Water also stands for charms, enchantments, poetry, the fine arts, and mystery. But it can also allude to self-sabotage and self-imprisonment.

Water can be murky where the fugitives of repressed emotions are hidden and safely locked away. Thus, the Waves can represent denial, dysfunction, and keeping secrets. With water, we can plumb the depths, but we may not be able to see the bottom. Most likely, we can never reach it. Water can be *that deep*. There are great riches and power behind the Waves, especially when the water breaks free, floods the dam, and wells up, reminding us of our deep, psychic connection with others. Water dissolves boundaries and tells us that we are *one*. Drawing the Waves Rune promises safety and protection since it reminds us of our beginnings in amniotic fluid in the sealed world of our mothers' bodies. Water holds our souls primeval.

At the present time you may feel more reclusive than usual, less willing to make a decision or a commitment. Instead, you may feel the need to withdraw into your own private world so you can reassess your losses and gather strength to once again face the world outside the womb.

The Waves Rune turning up in a reading offers mixed messages. You may be facing a period of turbulence or change where nothing is really steadfast. Now may be a time of low energy where you are unable to pinpoint your mistakes or to see who your real enemies are. This stone also implies that you are holding on to some idea or belief that is probably not true. Since the Waves are fluid and yielding, your path is now unsure. You can expect to receive cloudy and confusing messages that make it impossible to draw any conclusion, since you do not have all of the information you need. For whatever reason, the real truth is hidden, leaving you adrift. Yet, the Waves Rune has more positive implications—ones that are mainly spiritual.

Presently, you will not only be able to see and sense the divine in your life, you will also be able to attract the divine as well. More than any rune, the Waves Rune represents a quirky kind of celestial mysticism with stars, spells, smells, spangles, and midnight madness. When dealing with these subtle and mysterious forces, you are in your own element. After all, water mirrors the Sun, Moon, and Stars, which in turn mirror *you*: The symbol of waves implies self-reflection and a striving to find out what is genuine in your life.

At this time you will need to watch that you do not become the victim of some falsehood or intentional deceit. You should also be careful of going along with others just for the sake of belonging. Sometimes this can mean that you are not standing up for what you truly believe or know, or that you have no real integrity or opinions of your own. Despite the chaos, it's important that you remain as steadfast as possible now. In keeping with this, use caution regarding information that you are given at this time. Do what you feel makes the most sense, not what you think or feel you *should* do. Also, you need to make sure that you have not twisted crucial information to suit your own needs. It is essential that you remain true to your authentic self, not a false self that you or others have somehow created or embellished.

When the Waves Rune turns up in a reading, it can foreshadow a time of great psychic or artistic development. No matter what path you have chosen at this time, you will begin to notice and appreciate higher levels of reality that you may not have been aware of in the past. Expect unusual occurrences that will expand your consciousness or your outlook.

You may want to avoid becoming insular or secluded right now. You should avoid certain substances that make you feel better in the short term but can cause greater problems in the long run. Also, a good sense of timing is of critical importance to the matter you are asking about.

The Waves Rune represents both strengths and weaknesses. It indicates a period when you will feel overwhelmed, swept away by emotions and circumstances. You may feel that all of the energies you put forward tend to dissipate. It is important that you do not waver or lose faith.

Water indicates a certain kind of emotion and depth that is so compelling we are willing to drown in it and lose our souls in the process. It is the baptism of spirit and soul. With the Waves Rune, feeling rules everything. After all, it is water which draws us under so we can be born into a new life.

Waves Rune in summary   On the surface, this rune stands for intuition and the artistic imagination. But it also indicates cloudy perception. In this way, the Waves Rune can stand for self-sacrifice or self-sabotage. It means we are victims of our own delusions. There is the sense of not being able to pin something down, being left in suspension or being swept away by emotion or the imagination.

Other meanings behind the Waves Rune include a long trip or a voyage over water, events which are carried out in secret, mystical visions, healing herbs or magickal elixirs, dealing with perfumes or poisons, hidden agendas, groups which harbor secret or covert actions. When this rune turns up during a reading, it indicates that the answer is still not clear. Often, the matter of your concern will soon dissipate or phase out with no resolution or closure.

On the positive side, the Waves Rune represents a wellspring of creativity where you are nourished by the power of your own imagination. Sometimes this rune means that the matter you have asked about depends upon your timing. Poetry, music, and powerful revelations are behind the meanings of this stone. What you are able to imagine will soon become a reality, as long as you are willing to clarify what you ask for, and to follow through.

Scythe

You will be aware of an absence, presently,
Growing beside you like a tree . . .

Sylvia Plath

The Scythe and the idea of death have always been associated with negativity since death is what we fear. Yet the Scythe is a chilled wind, a bony hand of death that sweeps away that which has outlived its usefulness. It is no more evil or unnatural than the force that shakes crisp, autumn leaves to earth. After all, death is inevitable, but not final. This is why the Scythe has also been associated with the sign Scorpio and its governing planet Pluto: God of the underworld who drives the light of summer into the dark caves of winter. All dramatic transformations appear to be final but the wise ones know they are not. Spring always returns and so does life.

Whenever the Scythe Rune turns up in a reading, it suggests that it is time for a change. Perhaps you have been putting off bringing an end to a difficult situation because what you really fear is the unknown. This can be expressed in various ways, but the most obvious one is in relationships. It is likely that one key relationship needs to be phased out of your life or else the dysfunction will cut so deeply you will never be able to escape its negative ramifications.

On a mundane level, the Scythe Rune can indicate a divorce or a separation that does not end happily. Some of you need to ask yourselves if a short period of discomfort or unease is worth a lifetime of resentment? The worst thing you can do is cover up the obvious truth. Simply put, there is a danger here.

Important information may be concealed from you, rendering you incapable of making a decision based upon what you know. Now is the time to get to the bottom, to find the root cause, to reach that which is malignant or negative and then cut it out of your life. Only then can you expect real healing and a turn toward the positive.

The Scythe Rune has powerful implications. It can suggest events that shift your focus dramatically, forcing you to change or transform your strategy or plans. Often the Scythe Rune indicates that the question you are now posing is no longer appropriate, that things have changed too much to get the answer or outcome you are presently seeking. Thus, you must rearrange your thinking and ways of doing things. Sometimes this rune can suggest a meaning that only poses more questions.

All matters pertaining to the paranormal, especially ghosts and apparitions, the afterlife and reincarnation, have special significance. Therefore, you will be more keenly aware of the processes of both life and death, the concept of other realms and other existences outside of what is usually sensed.

If some of these ideas aren't worked out consciously, it is possible that you'll have some sense of foreboding or fateful loss which may or may not be real. In any event, it's likely that some action you have started will suddenly stop. It is even more likely that you will need to investigate what you are doing before continuing.

In keeping with this, you will notice that you have gained an ability to attract or repel various forces into your life since your powers of magnetism have been greatly enhanced. Be aware of a certain danger in aligning with these forces or energies as this could invite serious troubles you hadn't bargained for.

Since the Scythe corresponds to the sign Scorpio, it also suggests matters that have to do with taxes, trusts, wills, dealings with the goods of the dead, and rightful inheritances. Sometimes these assets will be hidden from you, such as property or materials belonging to ancestors that are rightfully yours. If so, you will probably need to go to an extreme effort to get them and will need legal help in doing so.

When the Scythe turns up in reaction to questions concerning relationships, it comes with a sobering warning and a word of caution. Beware of anyone who seems to want to use you—particularly your talents or connections—for their own purposes, to aggrandize themselves or better their own agenda. Beware of people who wish to sabotage your efforts in ways that are concealed. Look for groups or cliques ganging up in an effort to thwart your plans. Reading their motives may be difficult right now. You might think of their efforts as a heavy, velvet curtain. You can see that a team of persons is behind the curtain making it move but you cannot see who is pulling the strings. Be careful.

Metaphorically, the death experience represents the hero, the wanderer, the sojourner who dies and returns, bringing news from the next world and other realms. In this way you can expect your views, your realm of experience, to be completely altered by events that are unnerving and even shattering. There is no way to come to such wisdom and understanding without allowing some part of yourself to die. Have faith in the fact that you will have a second chance that will bring you a better way of life.

Scythe Rune in summary This rune means to cut away, to put an end to something, to sever or separate. Possibly something you have depended upon vanishes from your life. This can sometimes imply a divorce or a separation. Or it can simply mean that there is completion or closure. You can now move to the next level and begin anew.

When the Scythe turns up in a reading, this indicates certain changes must occur and time must pass before a reconciliation. It can mean you are coming to terms with something that is hard to accept. There may be a death, a will, a disappointment, a period of introspection after a loss. You may experience passing through difficulties, putting in time, a transformation, then reaching a new level.

The Scythe also represents various aspects of the paranormal, especially ghosts. Therefore, it can suggest the possibility of a ghost haunting your home or your life. The Scythe also stands for graveyards, sewers, and disturbing dreams.

Walls and blocks may seem insurmountable at the current time. But the Scythe implies you have the strength and fortitude to overcome all difficulties that you now encounter.

Eye

Do I contradict myself?
Very well then, I contradict myself;
I am large, I contain multitudes.

Walt Whitman

It was the Ancient Egyptians who first believed the eye was the seat of the soul. After all, eyes were the source of great power since they held not only the glimmer of our humanity, but our divinity as well. In the creation story of Osiris and Isis, it was their son Horus who restored the soul of Osiris by giving him the eye that had been plucked out by his wicked brother, Seth. Amulets were then made in the image of the Eye Of Horus, or *Udjat Eye* and used as charms and protection against dark forces. To the Egyptians, the Eye became the talisman of the Godhead or Goddess, as a burning presence of the divine. They associated the *Udjat Eye* with the fiery powers of sun and the reflective qualities of the moon. Coffins were painted with eyes—as watchers and guards over the bodies of the esteemed dead—on opposing sides of the casket. Eventually the Gypsies, who often touted themselves as Egyptians, brought the symbol of the Eye to the west as they rolled across European cities and towns.

While the Egyptians looked upon the symbol of the Eye favorably, later peoples associated the Eye with something much more foreboding. The Evil Eye is a universal idea in both the Old World and New World. Witches, and those with physical oddities, were said to possess a strange power or "cast," where a simple glance could bring ruin and misfortune on the unlucky person falling under their spell.

There is no evidence this was true. But it gave witch-hunters of the sixteenth and seventeenth centuries enough ammunition to fan the fears of a people whose beliefs were steeped in superstition. Hundreds of thousands of men and women were executed during this witch purge, although it is unlikely that most were actual witches. In fact, many of the those killed during the purge in Europe and America were Christian clergy, pillars of the community, innocent youth, and old widow women who did little more than own a pet or brew a healing tea. The witch hysteria became so great that "witches" were led into courtrooms backwards so they might not bewitch or "bind" the judge with their scalding gaze. The eye, after all, is the seat of the soul, and no doubt, such knowing looks were making the judges feel guilty.

It is even thought that bridal veils were first used in weddings to protect the bride and her future children from the envious stares of certain wedding guests. Around the same time, mirrors were used to break the spell of the Evil Eye—for if one could capture its reflection, one could blind it into submission.

The Eye is a very significant and awesome symbol among the Witch's Runes. In fact, when the Eye Rune turns up in a reading, it lends power and emphasis to the meanings of all other runes selected for interpretation.

So what does this important stone mean? The Eye Rune represents *perspective*, to have something brought into focus in such a way that you will never view things in quite the same way again. You can expect to get a sudden realization directly through the viscera, the very core of your emotions, rather than the gray matter of the brain. Such information may come to you as a shock, and also as an awakening. If not pleasant, this realization will certainly be life-altering.

The Eye Rune implies magick, incredible psychic powers, the ability to summon up what is yours, and the ability to change things by way of your own connections with some divine source. But perhaps magick is the wrong word. Your experience will be more of an attunement to the mysteries and energies of the universe. As a wise response to this call, the Eye suggests the power of the incantation, the chant, the blessing, and the prayer—the focusing on and mastering of one thing at a time.

In this way, the meaning behind the Eye Rune harks back to the motto of the Sun Rune: *One goal perfectly imagined, is one goal eventually achieved.* But the real message behind the Eye is even more urgent. It says: *Do it and do it now. If not now, then not ever.*

The Eye Rune has other important meanings along with personal magic and attunement to universal energies. It has to do with the soul's destiny, which is bound not only to the Creator, but also to other self-realizing souls on a similar path. In essence, the Eye Rune denotes the appearance of the soul mate soon to be a presence in your life—if he or she is not so already. Those who have been deeply in love at one time or another understand the spiritual implications that can be found in a romantic attachment. Some have said it is finding the God or Goddess in the other, which goes beyond physical attraction. Of course, if this were true, we would be soul mates with everyone we meet since the essence of the divine rests in all of us. It is only our desire to see divinity in our chosen mate that convinces us of the soul-mate relationship. Others believe that finding your soul mate is like gazing into a mirror, where edges blur, boundaries vanish, and the lovers unite as one.

So what is love? Perhaps it is the loneliness of the separated soul longing for itself. Perhaps it is the loneliness of the separated soul longing for heaven—if there is such a place. Perhaps romantic love is the closest thing on earth to standing in the presence of our creator's great and wondrous love. Thus, the Eye Rune not only represents the adoring eye of the lover whom we adore in kind, it is the adoring eye of our Creator whose love and light we wish to bask in throughout eternity.

In many respects, the Eye Rune says it is time to chart your own course and master your own fate. It suggests that now is the time for you to stand at the center of your universe and claim what is yours. In essence, the Eye Rune intensifies and magnifies the reading. It can represent the solitary being, which may be you, or another who is at a distance or estranged. The appearance of the Eye Rune can represent the soul becoming free of distractions and the usual limitations.

Since the Eye suggests watching or being watched, the turning up of this rune can predict a good amount of notoriety—fame or infamy. In other words, all eyes may soon be watching you! Learn to expect scrutiny, public interest, or being singled out for some special attention—*for better or worse.* Some need to be watchful of being stalked, followed, monitored and having their privacy violated. Others will simply enjoy the attention. Still others may find out that certain facts have been concealed from you, perhaps to undermine your success or power, or to protect you for your own good.

The Eye Rune is an affirmation of your current course of action, but you can also expect complications and difficulties. Here, there is temptation, because the Eye Rune can reward you with many ego strokes prematurely. Do keep in mind you should avoid any easy way out. Since your path is a high one, others will expect the very best of you. If you fall short, the ramifications could be quite defeating or discouraging.

The Eye Rune takes in the colors and the vastness of our world. The Egyptians knew that the seat of the soul does not rest within the heart. It rests within the eyes. Thus, our souls are wrapped up in our perceptions in the way we view our universe and beyond. As the artist Michelangelo pointed out centuries ago, genius exists in each and every one of us. But it can only manifest through the special vision of those who are wise enough to *see* and *find* it.

Eye Rune in summary This rune means to watch, to hold sway over, to be spellbound, to probe deeply and discover that which is hidden from view. It indicates magick, awakening the third eye, to become conscious and aware. This can sometimes mean that you will be shocked into some awareness.

WITCH'S RUNES AND ASTROLOGICAL
CORRESPONDENCES

Rune	Planet	Sign	Element
Sun	Sun	Leo	Fire
Moon	Moon	Cancer	Water
Flight	Mercury	Gemini	Air
Rings	Chiron	Virgo	Earth
Romance	Mars/Venus	Aries/Libra	Fire/Air
Woman	Venus	Taurus	Earth
Man	Mars	Aries	Fire
Harvest	Jupiter	Sagittarius	Fire
Crossroads	Saturn	Capricorn	Earth
Star	Uranus	Aquarius	Air
Waves	Neptune	Pisces	Water
Scythe	Pluto	Scorpio	Water
Eye	X	Yours	All elements

The Eye Rune implies the inner eye, to bring something into focus, to awaken or startle. It suggests the all-knowing or all-seeing consciousness. It represents hidden wealth, the presence of a great power, obsessions, the need to escape prying eyes, surety of purpose, secret projects and concealment.

This rune has everything to do with vision, including television, film, the optic nerve, psychic vision, clairvoyance, creative visualization, to see clearly, to examine, inspect, expose, and understand on the deepest level.

PART 4

Methods for
Reading the
Witch's Runes

$\mathcal{H}$ good way to start reading the Witch's Runes is to ask a specific question, ponder your question for a moment, then select a stone from the bag. After doing this, turn to the meanings of the runes in the preceding section and read carefully. You will no doubt be astonished with the results.

If you want a full psychic reading, one with more detailed information, you may want to use one of the methods of reading provided in the following section. Using different techniques will allow you to gain greater insight into the results the runes provide and will keep you from going stale as a reader.

It's a good idea to come up with your own reading methods if you are familiar with other types of divination or divinatory systems. If you know something about tarot cards, you can use tarot reading methods if you desire. My area of discipline is astrology, an ancient system based upon the movements of the stars. I use the runes in the place of signs and planets and it works out fine.

Throughout history witches have used all types of divination. An unfamiliar system such as the Witch's Runes can only be enriched by all of the others. The following are examples of ways to read and interpret the Witch's Runes.

Study them well and read on . . .

Asking a Question

When reading your Witch's Runes it is best to have a specific question in mind—at least to begin with. This is the only way to get a clear answer. If you are hard-pressed for insight into some troubling issues in your life, you might consider using the following reading techniques since they are simple and direct. Even if you're just curious about the outcome of a recent turn of events, using these methods can let you know of existing circumstances and what to expect.

Sit quietly and think of your question. Clear your mind of all emotional clutter and mental distractions. Try to think of nothing but your question. If you are posing a question for someone else, repeat the question aloud. Be as specific as possible. You will need to place your three runes in a row straight across. Reach into the bag and take out the first stone. Put the stone in the first position. Choose a second stone and place it in the second position. Carefully select your third stone and put it in the third position.

The first stone you choose sets the general tone of the reading. In Gypsy card reading, this placement represents the past or what has already been set in motion. The second stone is the present, or existing circumstances, *or* what will happen in a very short time following your reading. The third stone represents the future and should spell out the outcome—or will foreshadow the next series of events. Most important, you should put these elements together and synthesize their meanings instead of just looking at the runes individually.

Another remarkable way to read the Witch's Runes rather quickly is to ask a question and simply pull out one stone. You'll have to stay with this one rune. Remember, the most important element in getting a good psychic reading, especially one you give yourself, is to accept the truth and the reality of the situation.

Before continuing, let me give you the meanings behind the runes when asking specific questions. We will start with the Sun Rune.

SUN

Choosing this stone indicates an event of great importance and magnitude coming into your life. The sun is *numero uno* among the runes and is extremely fortunate in a reading. Currently, the forces are in your favor. However, personality conflicts may have something to do with the obstacles placed in your way. Expect to appear before the public or a crowd in some capacity. Coupled with the Moon Rune, the Sun can indicate that you may be moving soon. You can also expect to be challenged or scrutinized more than usual. Maybe you're getting talked about more than you'd like. However, for now, it's best just to enjoy the attention. Remember—you cannot please everyone. In the long run, you'll see that it's better than being ignored. So it's best just to please yourself. All in all, the Sun Rune is greatly positive. The presence of the Sun Rune indicates progress and taking the correct action. Under the sun, our brightest star, everything which can grow, will. (+)

MOON

Bad habits have led to an uncomfortable set of circumstances. This rune speaks of rash actions and everything going haywire for the time being. You've been ignoring some important pieces of information, or there's a pattern of falling into the same trap over and over again. Dreams, hunches and off-the-cuff remarks can lead you in the right direction. Strange forces, for better or worse, are at work behind the scenes. The Moon Rune also represents food, domestics, children, a pregnancy, nursing and nurturing, worry, negative thoughts, and weight gain. It stands for clandestine actions, scandal, secret love affairs, and being watched by a stranger. The Moon also gives psychic visions through dreams with exceedingly accurate results. You won't be able to approach things in the same way as you have in the past. The good news is, this will be for a relatively short period of time. Most positively, this stone stands for popularity. Generally, people will be more receptive to whatever you want to initiate or start. However, don't expect other people to act reasonable for the time being. Of course, this also includes yourself. (-)

FLIGHT

About this matter, you will hear news. Messages, letters, phone calls, and all methods of communication and contact will yield the results you're after. There is talk and lots of it. Papers are being shuffled and there are messages from afar. There is an urgent feeling to the Flight Rune. When selecting this stone, time is of the essence. Therefore, it is important to act now and not later. If you're waiting to hear from someone, do not despair. Word comes soon. This rune also deals with travels, especially air travel. Therefore, airlines or air mail may play a part in the final outcome of your question. Notes and other forms of writing, including signing important documents, will have something to do with this matter. (+)

RINGS

Now is not the time to go solo. This stone always represents some kind of team effort, whether it be a marriage, a business partnership, or the collective energies of a family. At any rate, expect help from a go-between or a significant other concerning this matter. Negative stones nearby can point to a marriage or partnership in serious trouble. However, combining forces is necessary in getting the results you're hoping for. A fussy person with trivial complaints may make the current situation even more difficult, so be on the lookout for him or her one. As far as your question is concerned, search for a partner or an agent who can help you make it work. (+)

ROMANCE

Although this rune denotes romance and sex, it has a deeper meaning behind the more obvious ones. The Romance Rune has to do with the bringing together of opposites, a reconciliation of opposing forces. This stone has a great deal of power behind it since it is imbued with the compelling energies of physical attraction and the procreative impulses. In this respect, the Romance Rune can give a jump start to anything that is already in place. It can also mean that the forces are aligning themselves in your favor. You can think of this as a project that is dear to you in some way, or a relationship you feel you must have. On the more negative side, the Romance Rune can represent jealousy and possessiveness, or a love affair gone sour. When drawing this stone, know that there is great power behind what you are currently initiating. Use this power wisely since it can backfire if used for selfish purposes. (-)

WOMAN

When drawing the Woman Rune, you can be sure a woman or a girl figures prominently in the outcome of your question. Depending upon the other runes you choose, this woman will help you achieve your goals, or she may be the one who opposes you. Since the runes are symbolic, of course, you can read various meanings in each of the stones. This stone represents art, nurturing, and creativity. It can indicate finding a niche where others will be supporters of your cause or sympathetic to your plight. The Woman Rune can represent the beginning of a goal or the birth of a project. This stone shows you rising above obstacles. In fact, the Woman Rune is good for clearing all kinds of negativity and opposing forces from your life. Expect a blessing. (-)

MAN

Of course, this stone represents man and the corresponding male energies. The Man Rune is wildly creative and assertive, but watch out for disruptive forces coming into your life right now, or a little later. Whenever this stone appears in a reading, it speeds up the outcome, implying a fast and unexpected change. Sometimes this outcome is surprising, or even a little shocking. Perhaps the results of your action are a little more than you bargained for. Selecting the Man Rune can indicate that you will soon be in the right place, defending your turf. You may have to be the enforcer, the initiator, the one who makes things happen. In essence, you will have to move quickly to get what you want. In fact, you probably should. Expect reckless abandonment, perhaps an accident, meeting up with a hothead or someone provoking you into action. The Man Rune also indicates action, responsiveness, and gaining a strategy. In short, expect a little chaos and lots of excitement. (+)

HARVEST

The Harvest Rune stands for ultimate fulfillment. This stone lends itself to many meanings, since it fits the particulars of the person asking the question. For the marriage-minded, it can mean an impending marriage or building a family. For those oriented toward business, the Harvest Rune can indicate big profits. For individuals interested in creativity, the world is their stage. For those interested primarily in spiritual growth, the sky is the limit. Whatever the question implies, there are big rewards, usually after long and enduring effort. With this stone, the good luck usually appears in threes—one amazing event followed by another and yet another. When drawing this rune, it suggests a period of time when things start to go your way. That is, if you trust it and make the appropriate plans. This positive energy should not be squandered on foolish pursuits such as unrequited love or a more impressive car. Save this good fortune for the really important pursuits and goals. Accept this fortunate turn and make it your own. (**+**)

CROSSROADS

Drawing this stone indicates obstacles are blocking your way. This is not all bad. It just means you will have to work a little harder and act wisely in order to get what you are now shooting for. The Crossroads, or "Crossed Spears" as they are sometimes called, indicate a turning point, but not without sacrifices on your part. Now is the time to pay your dues and it won't be easy. This rune also represents disagreements and quarrels. This stone is not very positive. This is definitely a testing period; you may even become unusually pessimistic at this time. But you need to remember that anything worthwhile is going to take some effort. And in the long run, the results will be longer-lasting and much more substantial. The Crossroads Rune indicates that you are now being called upon to question many troublesome areas and failed directions in your life. It may now be the time to cut your losses and move on to the next level. (**-**)

WAVES

The answer to your question isn't clear now. You may feel as if you are lost in clouds, smoky mirrors, foggy air. The real truth is in there, but lost somewhere! This is a time when things may feel right, but they probably aren't. The Waves Rune clouds the issue, making it difficult for you to see what is really going on. This can indicate a time when you are the victim of some form of deceit, or everyone knows what is going on except *you*. More positively, the Waves Rune symbolizes the evocation of spiritual forces of great power and mystery in your life. Divine happenings are at work and it is time for you to pay attention to them. The Waves Rune also means great glamour and allure, bringing public attention to whatever you do. It can also stand for a time when there may be deception, fraud, or misunderstandings. You may miss out on something because of bad timing. Things are not necessarily ill-fated, they are just confusing. It is probably best to turn your attention toward some kind of spiritual discipline. If you're an artist, the Waves Rune evokes a time of tremendous creativity and inspiration. At present, all forms of mind-altering substances should be avoided; however, your psychic ability should be greatly enhanced. In rare instances this rune can imply a haunting and the linking up with earthbound spirits, more commonly known as ghosts. In short, avoid self-indulgent activities but try to stay in good spirits. Cheers. (‑)

STAR

The Star Rune stands for a wish or a hope, but really it is what you yearn for. The Star Rune represents what you tend to elevate or hold in high esteem. It sometimes indicates a lifelong goal, or something that you are desperately seeking. The Star promises to enlighten or free you from dull circumstances. These are strange days, to be sure, but with fortunate results. There is the realization of hidden dreams and secret wishes where the spirit is nourished and the soul is fed. The Star, like the other runes, has a multitude of meanings. Turning up the Star Rune can indicate a gift of something precious, like a piece of jewelry or an engagement ring. The Star can indicate a substantial sum of money coming your way. The Star also represents dreams, traveling afar, and a quest much like the Magi following the star toward Bethlehem. Whenever the Star appears, you can be assured that wishes will be granted and dreams really will come true. (**+**)

SCYTHE

Always a warning, the Scythe Rune suggests that you should use caution concerning the matter you are now asking about. Once thought to be a bad omen implying danger, the Scythe simply represents a passage in your life when things will change dramatically and this is not always bad. The Scythe indicates the cutting away of something that frees you from bondage and eventual sorrow. Of course, this can represent painful life changes such as the break up of a marriage, moving out of a safe but dysfunctional relationship, or even a death—although this would be extremely rare. Now is the time to think things through carefully; do not take unwarranted risks.

Sometimes this rune can indicate the meeting of a rival or a formidable opponent. Beware of self-sabotage since your opponent may even be yourself. Jealousy or bad blood may be a factor in many of the obstacles that you now seem to face. The possibility of being cut off from something you feel is absolutely vital could be another unhappy element of this rune selection. Keep in mind, what is past has now passed away. There is no more time for regrets. (**-**)

EYE

What you have asked is destined, but it all depends upon how much energy you are willing to invest. In fact, now is a time when you will have to muster your own energies and go solo. This can sometimes indicate a lonely quest, where your efforts are misunderstood or thwarted. The Eye Rune can indicate fame, infamy, closed door sessions, information or secrets suddenly revealed that can change your course or direction. At present, you have the ability to command or sway decisions in your favor. It's time for you to use your inborn powers in a solo effort where the rewards are even greater than you dreamed possible.

The Eye Rune can also indicate a time when you are watched with interest and amazement. So expect to have your efforts discussed and talked about. However, rumours and gossip are likely to plague you. Being stalked, spied upon or hassled is a more negative form of this usually positive stone. What this rune really means is you have a great deal of power right now, and therefore, most people will tend to follow and support your efforts.

However, there are those who will respond to your newfound independence and confidence with jealousy and suspicion. More rarely, the appearance of this stone can indicate an element of danger or falling under someone else's influence. At worst, it stands for black magic, and even more conventional religious doctrines used in a destructive or mean-spirited way.

In olden times, this stone helped ward off the Evil Eye, as a protection against bewitchment, or the falling under a malevolent spell. In our present day, the Eye Rune represents the meeting up with a soul mate and also the maturation of your psychic powers. If you continue to act with integrity and honor, you can be assured that whatever you put into motion will most likely work out as planned, and probably even better. (✦)

Infusing the Runes with Your Own Meanings

Memorizing the meanings behind the Witch's Runes is just the beginning when it comes to using the stones and learning about their meanings. As with any type of divination, it is up to you come up with some of your own psychic solutions, as well as being sensitive to the many ways the stones speak to you.

With each question, each reading, the stones will begin to convey messages to the reader in a multitude of ways. For instance, the Flight Rune may not always mean "messages," it could also stand for a telepathic or spiritual connection. It could even indicate office equipment or an airplane ride. There is something of importance coming to you from a distance—somehow spirited through the air. What do you associate with flight and air? Use your better sense—your sixth sense, if you can. Likewise, the Star Rune may not always mean a goal or a wish, it might indicate light being shed on the truth. The Star is a steady light, so perhaps it could even mean the spotlight is now on you or the subject you question.

Tap your own genius. Use your imagination in ways only dreamed of before. Make the Witch's Runes your own.

Having a Dialogue with Your Stones

The more you use the stones, the more they will come alive, responsive to your every question or wish. One way of making the Witch's Runes truly yours and in tune with your energy is to sit quietly with the stones for a couple of hours. Pick up a rune and study it gently. Roll the stone in your palm and try to pick up the vibrations. Imagine sun, moon, and stars. Imagine nature. Imagine changes coming. Imagine your future.

You will know the stones belong to you when they begin to feel satiny and yielding in your palms. You may begin the feel an energy that is akin to the gentle rushing vibrations of water, or like a steady electric hum. Sometimes you will sense heat as if someone has held them close to a match. Or, the stones themselves may feel cold and flat instead, with only a tingling sensation in your hands.

Shift the stones from hand to hand. Juggle them carefully. Decide which hand you think the stones like best. Arrange the runes any way you like and stare at them for a long time. Memorize the symbols. Memorize the lines. Hold the stones like delicate, perfect eggs in your hands as if life is growing inside them. Think of how you nourish the stones with your attention and then imagine them nourishing you as well.

Slip the stones back inside their bag. For the next forty-five minutes or so, ask the stones a few questions. To begin with, try not to ask questions of any great importance. You and the stones are just getting to know each. Instead, test your runes a bit. You might ask them "What comes in the mail for me tomorrow?" or "What might this weekend bring?" Then, pull out a stone. Quickly write down your interpretation of what you believe the rune is telling you. Try to be a bit basic in your questioning for now. After a night or so of playing, you and your runes will become what you should be: old and familiar friends.

Getting Down to Brass Tacks: Yes or No?

When involved in a self-reading, or even a reading for someone else, it's possible to get a yes or no answer to your questions. As you may have noticed in the previous descriptions, there are positive (+) and negative (-) symbols at the end of the explanation of the stones. Positive runes indicate a yes answer, while negative runes mean a no answer. Keep in mind, getting a negative answer is not necessarily bad. Trends change, and oftentimes, a no answer only means that getting your wish will somehow be delayed. However, when the runes continually bring up negative answers, put them away for a while until you begin to feel some shift in mood.

When working with the stones, you must have your question clearly in mind. Avoid asking complicated questions, where the answer may be mixed. Try a simple approach, such as, Will I get the job I just applied for? rather than, What does my future employment hold? When you become more skilled at interpreting the stones, you can ask more ambiguous questions.

During the Yes–No reading, you are to select three stones. Ask your question aloud, and only then should you softly place your hand in the bag. Don't be anxious! Desperation and overenthusiasm can trick the psychic mind into seeing falsehoods as truth, since these emotions are so wrapped up in our neediness for the right answer—or at least, the answer we're hoping for. Touch the stones for a moment. Select the first stone when you begin to feel an energy buzz or the urge to choose. (You may want to set your rocks on a silky, black cloth. This will help you focus better.) Study the designs a little longer. But don't allow the images to flood your mind just yet. Pick another stone, and then, another.

And there you have it. Your own three stones. Look at the symbols. Do positives dominate? Or does your reading have more negative overtones? There are exceptions to this rule, you know. The Harvest or Sun Runes can completely override the negatives. Likewise, the Scythe Rune can overpower positive stones since with the Scythe there is always a warning.

The following are examples of recent readings I have given using my Witch's Runes.

A young man asked me about a trip he was about to take with his father and his father's fiancée. The boy's parents had been divorced since he was an infant. There was no real communication between his mother and father any longer since the divorce had been rather ugly.

Because the young man apparently felt awkward putting his hand in the bag, I chose the runes for him. The answer the stones revealed was unexpected and surprising. These are the runes I chose by random selection:

The first stone selected was the Moon, indicating the past, old hurts, memories, and self-sabotaging habits. The Moon also represents falling for the same traps over and over again. The second stone chosen was the Woman Rune. (Now this was getting interesting.) The third rune that turned up was the Crossroads, representing fierce opposition or an argument.

Not surprisingly, the boy never made the trip. His reading yielded all negatives and the Crossroads spoke of strong opposition to his going. In short, after much arguing, screaming, and threats, the boy's mother found other "more important" things for him to do while his father and the new woman in his life were enjoying the trip. Sadly, the boy's trip was sabotaged. And most amazingly, the Witch's Runes predicted this with uncanny accuracy.

A woman went to a writer's conference and met a famous poet whose writing she had always admired. Shyly, she approached him and they immediately struck up a conversation. There was an immediate bond. The evening turned out to be wonderful, and although the woman had to leave early, the poet noticed her leaving and waved warmly as she left the room.

About a month later, the aspiring writer wrote the poet a long, involved letter about her sadness and grief as a child, and how his writing had helped her a great deal. On a whim, she dropped her letter in a mailbox, but almost instantly regretted it. She was embarrassed over what she had confessed. Even more painful, was that months passed and there was no response.

I suggested we ask the runes about what this famous man had thought of her letter. With some hesitation, the woman agreed. Here is what turned up:

The first rune selected was, most appropriately, the Man Rune. This is a lively, energetic stone, even when there isn't a man involved in the meaning of the reading, so this was definitely a good sign. It indicated her letter was met with a certain intellectual excitement. The second rune was the Star Rune, also a positive omen since it represents secret wishes, lofty goals, dreams made real. The star is also what you yearn for, indicating ideal results. (Two out of three, so far. Not bad.)

The last stone that was turned up was Flight, predicting the poet would undoubtedly write back to the young woman and his response to her message would be a warm, friendly one. In fact, the stones were so positive, it was likely his message was being processed at that very moment in some way.

The outcome of the reading suggested that the woman's letter was met favorably and she would hear from the poet shortly. Six days later, she did. The poet apologized for not having written sooner, but explained he had been hard at work on an important book. His letter was filled with his usual generosity, humor, and compassion. As the Witch's Runes predicted, there had been absolutely no reason for the young woman to feel embarrassed, after all.

Very recently, an older friend contacted me to do a psychic reading for her. She said that she was desperate because she suspected that the woman she had hired to help her out was stealing items from her home. The friend admitted she felt terribly guilty for even thinking such a thing, because her housekeeper appeared to be a woman of great character and was the best and most efficient helper she'd ever had. But expensive objects were suddenly missing. In fact, my older friend said she didn't know how she could possibly get along without the woman. "Please tell me it isn't so," were the last words my friend said before hanging up the phone.

Before beginning the reading, I checked my trusty calendar and planetary guide to make sure the moon wasn't void-of-course. I always do this when attempting a really serious reading, especially in situations where someone's job is at stake. The same is true when handling cases of missing persons or other serious matters. A void-of-course [unaspected] moon can sometimes skew the accuracy of a psychic reading. However, a few rare psychics actually prefer the moon when it is void, claiming it increases clairvoyance and gives them greater focus.

Then I pulled out my bag of Witch's Runes and began the reading. Here are the stones that turned up:

The first stone selected was the Scythe Rune, which did not bode well for the innocence of the woman. In fact, this rune often suggests that the relationship in question needs to be cut off immediately for the betterment of all involved. The Scythe, which corresponds to the astrological sign of Scorpio, indicates secretive or covert activities. The second stone that came up was the Eye Rune. The Eye usually indicates that a person is being watched or monitored, and in this case, the woman *was* monitoring her housekeeper. But even more likely, the housekeeper was monitoring the older woman's comings and goings so she'd have a prime opportunity to pilfer more loot. The third stone selected was a bit of a surprise. The Harvest Rune indicates the need to gain or profit through actions previously described. The older woman mentioned that some of the items missing had been purchased in Europe many years before and could not be replaced. There was little doubt in my mind that the housekeeper was taking these precious possessions and selling them out-of-state for a hearty profit. No doubt, for a little while, this "lady" was in hog heaven.

I called my friend back and gently delivered the news. She was disappointed, but thanked me for my help. A few weeks later, the older woman opened up a bill from one of her credit cards. Stunned, she read down a column of figures where nearly $2,000 worth of merchandise had been charged to her credit card. The only other person with access to her card was her housekeeper. When confronted, the housekeeper confessed her guilt, but in a cool manner that showed no remorse. Shortly thereafter, the woman was fired. Later it was learned the same housekeeper had testified at a murder trial where she knew of a murder, but did not report it—eerily echoing the meaning of the first stone drawn—the Scythe. The cutting off, represented by the Scythe, implies an end to the matter. In rare instances, it can even mean death.

The previous reading methods are simple and to the point, but this doesn't mean you can't improvise and come up with your own ways of reading the Witch's Runes. These stones belong to you and the best way to learn to read the symbols is by building your own world around them. You may even come up with more rich and diverse meanings than I, or witches from ages past, have ever even dreamed about. After all, every creation, every belief, every germ of a new idea begins with a dream, either sleeping or waking. A dream in the mind of a human is a cosmic seed reaching into heaven. And, as all us witches know, attuned to moon and night: *the dream goes on forever.*

Rune Combinations

Astrologers know that when two planets come together to form what is called a *conjunction*, the energies from the two planets will create a third energy that is related yet distinct from the two original planets. Poets know that when they compare two seemingly unlike things in a poem, a third meaning will be borne out of this *metaphor*, one that is related, yet distinct from the two original meanings. Everyone knows that when a man and woman come together, if the energy is right, a child will emerge from the *bond*, who is related, yet different from the two original parents.

The same could be said of the Witch's Runes. When doing a reading with the runes, it is of utmost importance to read the stones together, and to not separate their meanings. For instance, the Scythe Rune would carry with it a sense of foreboding if it turned up beside the Crossroads. However, if the Scythe came up with the Harvest Rune and the Star Rune, this reading would actually be mostly positive. Likewise, the Sun Rune would be positive, unless it fell between the Scythe Rune and the Crossroads Rune, which could indicate cataclysmic events.

The following are some examples of meanings behind the runes as they fall in conjunction with each other. Of course, these are simply suggestions. As soon as you get used to reading your Witch's Runes, you will, in fact, uncover meanings entirely on your own. In other words, it's important to find your own meanings and allow your intuition to flow.

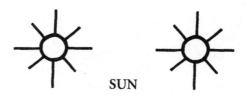

SUN

Sun/Moon Both of these runes are greatly positive since they indicate success, victory, bold transformations, or transitions. You can look forward to a sudden shift or a startling change of events that will alter or change the way you view the world and yourself. You can expect dramatic developments surrounding your job, your long-term career, your family, and where you live. This combination of runes suggests all manner of attention will soon be focused upon you and your goals. You can also expect to meet someone who sweeps into your life and mesmerizes you. The only negative aspects to these stones are possible vision problems or disturbances that may require medical attention.

Sun/Flight Get ready to go! You can look forward to distractions, free-flowing talk, gossip, important messages, poltergeists, problems with noise or sounds, and situations involving some type of electronic media. Other possibilities may be that you will become involved in the promotion of yourself, your creations or ideas, or the ideas of someone else in the very near future. Concerning your question, distances must be crossed in order to make this goal a reality. You would do well to seek out situations that involve travel, flight, or long distances. Expect activity, excitement, and moving around quite a lot. There is news coming which is probably the news that you are looking for.

Sun/Rings Be prepared for a wedding, a proposition, or an announcement that sends the room spinning. Crowds gather for social events. Expect laughter, levity, and whimsical actions. You may want to avoid that which is superficial by getting down to bottom-line issues. You would also do well to join your energies with that of a partner or friend in order to achieve your objective. You will soon need to be on the lookout for a charming individual who tries to get on your best side by using flattery or simply by bragging. It's doubtful anything serious will develop and you can consider this unusual encounter a learning experience. You can also look for important contacts that could turn into big *contracts.*

Sun/Romance   This rune combination foretells the sparking of sexual or romantic interests, a close bond, the airing out of passions, or an affair. Any endeavor at the present time will take two or more to make it a success. Keep in mind, sex appeal or attractiveness will have something to do with the outcome of this reading. The combination of these stones presents a strong energy to deal with since it gives a significant amount of tension and power to any reading. However, when using this power, your motives must be pure. You would also be advised to put all of your cards on the table and leave things aboveboard. Any subversive plans or plots would surely backfire and create an ugly scene. It's important that you make an exemplary presentation at this time since much depends upon your personal appeal and how you come across to others. In addition, sexuality, whether by gender or preference, could be an issue.

Sun/Woman   You can look forward to lavish pursuits, high ideals, indecision, romance, and creativity of all kinds. Some who draw these stones will visit a building, possibly an office, devoted to spirituality, the law, or the fine arts. Others may find themselves left in charge of social affairs, entertainment, or creative projects. The vibrations of the above runes are warm and flowing, but they are not specific. Yet magickal events are surely at work behind the scenes, and you would do well to hook up with this kind of life-enhancing and creative energy. You may soon find yourself acting in a teaching capacity or as a leader or a guide. It's possible that a female will hold the power in this situation. In short, you should be able to achieve your objective with ease as long as the other runes are favorable.

Sun/Man This rune combination has an explosive quality and speeds everything up to a frenzied pace. Look for reckless behavior, a battle of wills, self-sabotage, hostile actions, or difficulties with authority figures. The Man Rune represents action, and the Sun Rune reveals what is pressing you at the current time. You would be advised to avoid dangerous situations and stick with calmer activities at the moment. Plus, you might as well forget leading or organizing another group of people anytime soon. They will only fight you, leaving your efforts and plans frustrated. Look for your activity level to pick up greatly. Also look for several exciting but unnerving developments concerning your question in the next few days. Understand that all may not be positive and some results will seem shocking.

Sun/Harvest This grouping is enormously positive. There are definitely good tidings here. In this position, you can expect the Sun Rune to shine brightly upon all that you have recently accomplished or have poured energy into (or soon will). The Harvest Rune represents the big payoff, the reward, or the prize after everything else has been said and done. You can expect the results to be in your favor— but only if you complete your task. However, in cases where fate does not deliver the results as planned, you can expect surprising benefits to lead to a new direction that is probably better than what you first had in mind. What you accomplish right now will only expand and multiply. Be prepared for better luck.

Sun/Crossroads This can be a bad omen. Thus, be on the lookout for treachery, obstacles, blocks, or serious opposition. The Gypsies saw the crossroads as indicative of arguments or sabotage. The Sun Rune only enhances this meaning, indicating that you must now use extreme caution and also look for signs that currently surround you. Look for enemies or opposition to be brought out into the open. Expect pressure from those who think they-know better than you do. One step forward, two steps back. If you are wise and crafty, you can use this solid but stoic energy to your benefit. All in all, you will need to be careful at the present time.

Sun/Star The outcome of your reading is mostly positive, but these are strange days. Although events should progress in a positive way, they will not go according to plan. You can expect mix-ups that could delay matters, forcing you to change your present course of action. Some may meet an eccentric or an unusual person who delivers a profound piece of information. Others may be put into the spotlight because of their uniqueness or differences. Some will make important spiritual connections by using an unconventional approach. Others may need to master more complicated skills and techniques in order to achieve what they're after. Seek out the right help and greater precision concerning your goals.

Sun/Waves This is a mysterious combination that foretells psychic messages, ocean travels, fantasies, and dreams. This rune combination has very much to do with the art of deception, but this is not always bad. It all depends upon whether you are meeting up with fine artists, con artists, or something in between! Whatever the case may be, you can look for the outcome of your question to turn out cloudy or unresolved, leaving you waiting, or just disappointed. Expect to be left hanging in midair, unable to make any move forward. It will seem as if other people are not as serious you are or are very irresponsible. This rune combination has much to do with nighttime, secret rendezvous, and troubled sleep. Think of prowlers, Peeping Toms, cheating hearts, and insomniacs. Think graveyard shift. As a poet once wrote, "This is the stuff dreams are made of." Yet dreams fade in the morning light. Draw another stone for more clarity.

Sun/Scythe   There are great powers at work here, but you need to proceed with caution. Drawing the Scythe always foretells the end to something. But often when the Sun Rune appears alongside the Scythe, it is not always obvious what should end because of the optimistic, feel-good quality of the Sun Rune. However, if you search the dark recesses of your soul, no doubt you will realize the painful truth. Something you have depended upon or have taken for granted is coming to an end. It's best to walk softly because your field of dreams may end up a field of booby traps. The Scythe Rune is rather treacherous and represents endings. All things must pass. Expect a decision, but perhaps not in the way that you had hoped or wished.

Sun/Eye   This rune combination has enormous magnetism. In many ways, this means that you are the master of your own ship. You now have the strength to accomplish what you need. Perhaps you are being watched, judged, or scrutinized. Perhaps it will be you who leads the pack this time. Think stage, arena, movie theater. Think crowded room. Look for excitement and thrilling developments. Hold fast to your values. Amazing forces are at work behind the scenes. The results are aligned in your favor.

MOON

Moon/Flight   This rune duo corresponds to the Goddess of mysterious darkness, Hecate, and her wise owl who delivers messages from the world of sleep and dreams. Some who turn up these stones may experience disturbing dreams, odd sleep patterns, or suffer from bouts of insomnia. Others may be awakened to startling news. Concerning your question, a person with special knowledge or vision should help you find your answer. Also, you won't be able to figure things out in a mental way right now. It's better to rely upon your intuition and worry about the hard facts later. If you depend only upon the facts, this could lead you in the wrong direction. Learn to read actions rather than words. Telepathy, ringing telephones, misdirected communications may figure in the matter you are posing.

Moon/Rings This is not a very dynamic rune combination, therefore you should not expect quick developments. In fact, this combination can indicate that your question is no longer relevant, and you need to rethink a few things before asking again. If your question is pressing you, you may be disappointed to learn that this issue will probably fizzle out before anything really substantial is gained. This combination can indicate a long engagement or an affair that seems to go on forever without real change or growth. It can mean that many of your efforts are being taken for granted, or that you are not getting any reward for the energy you have invested. Maybe you are attached to something old or something you've outgrown. Now's the time to make a switch. Now's the time to be a risk-taking witch.

Moon/Romance This is a more positive rune combination since it has a sexual energy behind it indicating the powers of attraction. But keep in mind, this does not always mean sex! It can actually indicate the push and pull of personal magnetism, or power struggles. Right now, you will feel a great deal of energy behind most of your pursuits. Perhaps some of these may be romantic in nature. If so, this combination suggests instant attractions that can turn into addictions. The good news behind these runes is that you will find it easier to go after long-term goals without being distracted by the trivial. In fact, you may notice that you have greater powers of concentration. But you will need to steer clear of any kind of obsessive thinking as this will surely defeat your purposes.

Moon/Woman Usually this rune selection indicates a kind, nurturing woman or one who has come into your life to teach you something of significance. Since the Moon represents time gained or lost, you can expect to make changes in your schedule or plans. You may completely change your course of action or career by choosing work that is closer to home and family. Your mother, wife, sister, daughter, or an aunt may figure in the matter you are now posing. Female relatives will be of importance or concern. More rarely, these runes can mean you end up isolated in your home or from your family. Look for emotional bonding and linking up with female forces.

Moon/Man   These stones can represent someone who is ill-tempered, indicating circumstances that are irritating, emotionally volatile, or at the least, quite upsetting. You can expect to encounter a very difficult person who tries your patience, or someone who forces you to act in an ugly way that is not typical of you. You may experience extreme restlessness, the flaring up of anger, or the surfacing of hostilities. You should also be aware of the possibility of exerting too much pressure or force on someone else, or becoming the victim of his or her lashing out. Speediness and haste may lead to accidents, so move slowly. You may be put on the spot to make a decision you'd rather avoid. Move slowly and use caution.

Moon/Harvest   These runes by themselves are an excellent combination as they indicate abundance and easy flow. Everything is right here. *It will happen* as long as you are willing to follow through. But this can be a big *if* since the Harvest Rune can sometimes denote extravagance and the tendency to let things slide. However, all in all, this is one of the best combinations of runes, since you will feel many of the obstacles that have held you back being lifted, or you may find yourself turning your life around. Your best projects will continue to expand and bear fruit. This brings up the possibility of pregnancy! If this isn't what you want right now, be careful.

Moon/Crossroads   This combination is not very favorable because it suggests that whatever you try to do at present will be blocked by the efforts of people who wish to defeat you. At this time, you may feel more discouraged than usual and you may sense that other people are treating you with an emotional chilliness or indifference. Therefore, it will be tough to keep your confidence up for the moment. Issues from the past may resurface and you will have to deal with them in a different way than before in order to resolve them. Problems having to do with the elderly, health, or age differences may also appear. Look for obstacles, friends who are not really friends, frustrating circumstances, feeling wounded, bad vibes, quarrels, and serious faux pas.

Moon/Star This rune combination represents speculation, the realization of dreams, goals, and long-range plans. The moon and stars light up the night skies, symbolic of the dreams that are clearly visible but also beyond our grasp. At the current time, you will be given a direction, a way in which to achieve your dreams. But you need to look at this as a beginning and not as the end. There is more work up ahead. To stay the course will not be easy, since you may experience many distractions and diversions along the way. You can look at it in this light: The sky is opening up for you. It's important that you not allow this time of positive growth to slip through your fingers without taking advantage of the opportunities. You can expect to stumble upon a lucrative idea, a breakthrough that leads you in the right direction. Others may experience unexpected blessings. For some, there will be a parting of ways or a separation.

Moon/Waves Your imagination may be strong but your focus is unclear. It is not a good time to be lax or allow things to happen on their own. This combination can mean that you have misjudged something, or perhaps you have acted at the wrong time—either too soon or too late. The Moon and Waves Runes suggest powers of clairvoyance, and it may be that you are gathering information in an intuitive way. This can create very loose boundaries for your psyche. Thus, you are now quite impressionable, and therefore easily led. There could be a denial of what is real, a twisting of the truth. Perhaps you are clinging to something that ended long ago. More positively, these runes can represent traveling overseas as a way of enriching the mind and the soul.

Moon/Scythe   This is a difficult position, but it is also very powerful. The Moon/Scythe energy depends upon how well you choose to use it. This can mean that in order to move on with your life, you will have to tear down many issues that have plagued you since childhood and you will need to reassemble them to fit your present needs. In this way, you must create a new structure or foundation by building from the ground up. You may also feel that others are exerting pressure on you in order to manipulate you for their own purposes. Thus, you will have to make serious changes in your relationships as well. Some may experience difficulties with women, while others will need to address troubles within the family. Right now, you can expect others to misunderstand your actions. Some may even join forces to block you. The more mundane meanings behind these runes have much to do with the Moon and Pluto, including graves, gutters, the past, memories, and life-and-death issues. To be led by your passions at present could put you in peril.

Moon/Eye   Consider gaining a different perspective at the current time. Never underestimate this combination since it represents the awesome power of spiritual forces. You may be the victim of haunting, or you may have to resolve a situation through your own psychic awareness. These runes also indicate an intense bond between two people who are separated by distance, years, or even death.

FLIGHT

Flight/Rings   This combination suggests courting or wooing by using sweet talk or kind words. of course, this can bring light verbal manipulation and flattery that is disingenuous. Thus, you will need to pay attention to actions and results rather than words, in order to draw the right conclusions. You can expect ease in all kinds of communications, romantic intrigues, or a flirtation. You can look for a letter involving shared property, a proposal of marriage, a marriage of minds, a contract that involves common goals, legal papers or documents and that which pertains to joint interests.

Flight/Romance   Prepare for messages of a romantic nature, a sexual proposition, phone calls or messages from prospective amours, or learning of a love affair. This combination can also indicate a crush or an infatuation that never really develops into an actual romance. Some may hear news that is startling or learn about a surprising scandal. This combination is interesting because it implies a sexual charge to the matter in question. This should give you insight into where you now stand. Be on the lookout for aggressive pursuits and sexual teasing. It won't be boring.

Flight/Woman   You can look for an important message coming your way that will be signed by a woman. Concerning the matter of your question, a female will act as go-between or agent to insure the success of your current goals. This combination also suggests that it is an excellent time to buy, sell, or trade domestic properties such as a home, a family car, clothing, or items of furniture. Look for major communications or connections involving a female. In the final analysis, a woman will have the last word. A woman is your answer here.

Flight/Man   Loose words or impulsive deeds may lead to misunderstandings. Expect arguments, disagreements, or hostile words coming your way. More positively, look for fast communications that will be the deciding factors concerning your question. Everything picks up and progresses quickly. It's a good time to get things in order, since circumstances will develop a lot faster than you expected. But you may need to watch out for recklessness or foolhardy actions. Arguing over the phone or harassing phone calls are other manifestations of this rune combination. But in most cases, they are no big deal.

Flight/Harvest   Excellent news should be coming your way. Blocks, which have slowed your progress, should be less of a problem. This will enable you to move forward and get the job done after previous stops and starts. Through the mail, phone lines, computer lines, or faxes, you should get word of something that will completely alter your current path to something far more lucrative. This will be especially true in the case of career advances or professional agreements involving finances or trade. Communications of all kinds will be of benefit now. This is a lucky combination for writers or those who work in communication fields like television, radio, or computer services.

Flight/Crossroads   Proceed with more caution, especially in areas of communications. The turning up of these two runes can indicate fighting, slander, or quarrels. Sometimes this means you will run into uncooperative or uncouth people. It can also mean that you will not be able to really express what you think at present for various reasons. You may want to be careful with any documents you sign as these could eventually require more energy or attention than you care to invest. At any rate, misunderstandings are likely, so stay cautious. Agreements made at the current time will probably not turn out as expected.

Flight/Star   This combination is definitely a bright spot as it indicates the crystallization of long-range goals and plans. Look for a message or letter that will not only excite you, but also change your course or direction. Papers and documents bring on opportunities that promise to open up your world. Air travel or long distance phone calls are likely concerning this matter. A sense of daring helps you overcome limitations. Any bold step should benefit you now.

Flight/Waves You will need to be precise, since all communications are not what they appear to be right now. Be suspicious of any grand claims. Keep in mind, your *fakirs* may actually be *fakers*. Do not be led astray by pie-in-the-sky claims or unfounded information. You should probably not make any key decisions until you have all the details. Some of you may become involved in psychic communications where you encounter the presence of ghosts and spirits. Others may experience odd psychological states such as falling into a trance, autism, hypnosis, or the inability to concentrate. The positive manifestation of these runes suggests creative talent for writing novels or poetry, since these stones suggest the stringing together of beautiful words. In fact, this is a lucky combination for literary types and musicians.

Flight/Scythe Prepare for a message cut short, a visit missed, a loss, or a disappointment. It's also a time for strange intrigues, rumors, and keeping secrets. Some may experience feelings of unease, fall victim to chronic worrying, or will learn something that is highly disturbing. Others may become aware of a scandalous situation that occupies all of their attention or energy. Some may be shocked by crude language or unwanted advances. Jealousy could be one factor in the matter you inquire about. Turning up these runes imparts a warning that it's probably not a good time to be too trusting of certain relationships. Although Anne Rice's vampires are fictional, psychic vampires are very real. If you begin to feel tired often, you may need to reevaluate some of your friendships. More positively, expect powerful, life-altering communications.

Flight/Eye Enormous force and fated events are behind your question. It's possible you are being watched, admired, or scrutinized. You should hear word *from* or *about* a soul mate—possibly one at a distance. Expect a piece of news that will completely change your course of action—you get the green light on a new direction.

RINGS

Rings/Romance   This is a favorable combination for all kinds of relationships, especially those based upon romantic attractions. It is a positive sign for those searching for greater commitment and security from their partners. In essence, this combination suggests the cementing of important bonds and associations. Also, some can look forward to a celebration, an engagement party, an announcement, or an anniversary. Others will benefit from joint ventures and romantic attractions.

Rings/Woman   You can expect your luck to come by way of a woman. Concerning your question, you can look forward to the lifting of obstacles and greater ease in achieving your desires. Naturally, a female should play an instrumental part in this situation. Light and joyful activities should be coming into your life. This is a lucky combination.

Rings/Man   You may be feeling tension from partners at the current time, although this is not necessarily bad. You will need to be on the lookout for power struggles and possibly arguments within a marriage or a partnership. Things will probably not go according to plan, and so you will probably need to change your approach. However, this can be a fortunate position as long as you are willing to work with people, and not be so much on your own. It is not a good time to rock the boat. Concentrate on harmony and acceptance.

Rings/Harvest   Again, this combination is beneficial to those already committed to a key relationship. Those who are not involved romantically can expect benefits from joint ventures or assets and, generally, greater flow and ease. Pregnancy is possible for some. Others may just add additions to their homes.

Rings/Crossroads Marital difficulties or strife in partnerships are likely at this time. Arguments and misunderstandings are a likely scenario at present. Beware especially of treachery!

Rings/Star A gift, a precious item that is meant to be yours, a small piece of jewelry, an heirloom, accolades, or a small sum of money may be coming your way. The possibility of winning an award or a prize exists, but usually from hard work rather than from lucky breaks. Important messages come your way by phone or other types of electronic media.

Rings/Waves Inspired relationships and the appearance of a soul mate coming into your life are indicated here. For some, this may simply mean that another person shows you some kindness or grants you a much needed favor. Some will experience more sensitivity to poetry, beauty, and art. Unfortunately, this can mean you are not very grounded in reality at this time. Therefore, you must beware of deceit in relationships, hidden actions, illicit affairs, or just being lied to because others believe you are not able to handle the truth.

Rings/Scythe This combination indicates a close but somewhat unhealthy bond between two people. Expect the possibility of jealousy, intrigue, possessiveness, or even infidelity in relationships. Unnatural closeness, emotional manipulation, or smothering may play a part in the circumstances you are now asking about. A separation, divorce, or estrangement is possible between intimate friends or partners. More positively, you should soon link up with an unusually powerful person.

Rings/Eye You can look forward to compelling attractions and cutting-edge developments. This rune combination can be summed up by one word: infatuation. You can expect the meeting of kindred spirits, those who seem linked to you in some unexplainable way. You may find yourself being watched intently or becoming infatuated with someone who seems to be the answer to your dreams. You can expect others to seem suspicious or skeptical, but you can also look forward to being cherished and admired.

ROMANCE

Romance/Woman Obviously, this combination implies a strong physical attraction and is indicative of some kind of romantic pursuit. Even if you are not looking for romance right now, this rune can suggest unconscious sexual or romantic motivations. Sometimes this can mean a crush or some kind of light but gentle flirtation going on where nothing really develops. Look for sexual intrigues or finding an escape through romantic diversions. These stones also indicate appeal to the opposite sex and a warm, charming charisma.

Romance/Man You have begun to feel very impatient about several areas of your life. This combination suggests a sexual impulsiveness that could lead to promiscuousness. Most definitely, these runes predict some kind of hot pursuit. You can expect several areas of your life to be energized and actions surrounding these circumstances should pick up considerably. Concerning your question, the outcome should come about more speedily than expected. Therefore, you should make plans to move quickly and strike while the iron is hot.

Romance/Harvest This combination is very fortunate. The combination of the Romance and Harvest Runes indicates a good sense of timing and the ability to act decisively with a greater feeling of confidence. For some, this can mean a once-in-a-lifetime love affair, or one that will be greatly beneficial to your financial or social status. You can expect ease and good vibes. A person you know may act very generously toward you because of some kind of unconscious sexual attraction. In some instances, this may even be a person of the same sex. You will also find that people will be more willing to work with you toward a common goal. The only bad news is you may notice others tending to exaggerate.

Romance/Crossroads Combined, these runes indicate a turning point in key relationships. You may notice lovers or friends growing distant or cold. Perhaps you will embark on a more meaningful path. But you may feel paralyzed or discouraged, since all paths appear to have major obstacles blocking your dreams. In retrospect, you will see the path you chose is not as hard as you'd imagined, and you will accomplish most of what you had hoped. However, only romances meant to last will endure this troubling period.

Romance/Star The grouping of these two runes represents *conception* on every level. Possibly you will become involved in the conception of a lucrative idea, or a concept that broadens the awareness of others. And some, more rarely, may be involved in the conception of a child. With regard to your question, there is the sparking of something new, a beginning. Those involved in romances may be frustrated over a lack of commitment, or just a general sense of dissatisfaction and wanting to move on to a different, more stimulating affair.

Romance/Waves Concerning your question, you will not be able to count on it. Part of this stems from the fact that nothing substantial has been agreed upon. Plus, whatever has been decided upon—if anything—will probably dissolve or dissipate, leaving you holding the bag. Look for false information and confusion. What you are saying and the energy you are putting out is not understood. Be clear.

Romance/Scythe Romance, in general, offers challenges. This grouping of runes suggests the severing of a bond, a parting of ways. You can expect the end to key relationships in which you carry a lot of emotional baggage. Many of these separations will seem painful, but you will begin to come alive again after they have phased out of your life. Look upon this period as a fresh chance or new birth. Take the initiative and build a strategy. Make things happen in your life instead of just letting life happen to you.

Romance/Eye You are being watched with interest, your movements enjoyed or scrutinized. The appearance of this rune combination implies fated events, karmic associations, and special bonds. Some need to beware of falling victim to sexual obsessions or fantasies that steer them off course. Others will need to make sure relationships do not distract them from important goals. At any rate, you can expect telepathic, soul-level bonds that carry across the distance. Avoid triangles, romantic intrigues, or people who keep their motives hidden. Just allow the spirit of love to carry you—here, there, and everywhere.

WOMAN

Woman/Man This rune combination suggests opposing influences surfacing in your life. Although this selection is not necessarily negative, you can still expect your efforts to be blocked, or you may experience an inability to act because of frustrating obstacles. You may notice friction in relationships where people work toward cross purposes. This combination also represents a man and a woman working as a team and discussing the issues. Therefore, a couple may wield influence concerning this matter.

Woman/Harvest You can look for an act of great generosity coming your way, possibly through a woman, but more specifically, someone who has your best interests at heart. Relationships of all kinds should improve shortly and you may experience financial gain or relief during this period of greater ease and flow. Some can look forward to a new love relationship while an old one phases out.

Woman/Crossroads This rune selection can be quite troublesome, since it represents quarrels, battles, and various conflicts. This can indicate rivalry, arguments, troubles between women, or just a nasty person kicking up dirt. Whatever your question, you can expect *an end to something* that was probably not good for you in the first place. Other factors include the avoidance of important issues, psychic vampires, pests, or a person who uses weakness to control others. You can also expect an authority figure to pressure you in a negative way.

Woman/Star Wherever there is the star, there is elegance, idealism, and unconventional beauty. A lucky combination, this selection of runes foretells prizes, awards, accolades, recognition, and some miraculous turn of events. With the star, there:are spiritual awakenings as well as a longing for change. Don't muddy the waters. It's important to clarify your visions.

Woman/Waves A wellspring of creativity, the mind is filled with many fertile ideas. Some will have experiences of telepathy and clairvoyance, while others will decide on a completely different direction. Sometimes this combination can mean you are not getting the correct information, either through intentional deceit or petty misunderstandings. You need to be careful that you do not miss something through distractions or by not giving enough attention to detail. Fanciful escapism could leave you holding the bag. Avoid negative people at this time.

Woman/Scythe The Scythe always means the death of something, the tearing down of the old, and then the building back up; therefore, you can expect a great deal of dramatic change. You can look forward to the residue of an unhappy past being cleared away for new action, a fresher perspective, and also hope. Some may end up feeling betrayed by a friend, or a person they believed to be either benevolent or harmless. In essence this rune combination indicates masked hostility where someone is hurting you, but you don't know why, and often you cannot imagine who. Now's the time to stand strong and defend your principles and interests. It's also time to figure out who your enemies are and to name them. Otherwise they will continue to work against you.

Woman/Eye   Concerning this matter, you now have the ability to influence and master your own fate. Whatever happens depends entirely upon you and how much energy and fortitude you are willing to invest. This rune selection also suggests a person coming into your life who will transform it, for good or evil. The end result is not now clear. At any rate, you can expect meeting a powerful female with unusual spiritual gifts.

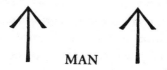

MAN

Man/Harvest   You can expect things to pick up considerably. It's a good time to launch a new action or set the wheels turning. Look forward to speedy progress with the question you are now posing. You will want to jump at opportunities since now is the time when you have the right energy to get things done. This is not a good time to gamble or attempt something risky, however. Interactions with males should be fortunate, as long as sexual affairs are avoided. This rune selection can represent fertility for all involved.

Man/Crossroads   Generally, this is a bad omen, but it's important not to become fatalistic when this combination turns up. One meaning behind these runes suggests that you will want to force things to happen too quickly, or you may pressure someone at an inopportune time. It can mean that as soon as you exert pressure, everything will explode and you'll be worse off than you were before. This can also mean that an enemy or a rival will choose to oppose you openly. Do be careful.

Man/Star Expect a bumpy ride and rough terrain. You can also look for unusual and startling developments concerning your question. Whatever happens will surprise you to your very essence. Such an experience may upset, jolt, or awaken you. But in the long run, you will see that the shocks you are now going through will work out better than what you initially had in mind. Keep it open for now. Things are not as they appear.

Man/Waves This combination means hidden troubles and unseen circumstances. With this selection, there are tangled vines and intrigues. Look for indirect hostility and aggression. Look for sneakiness and covert actions. This combination can imply that someone is angry with you, but somehow cannot face you. This can also suggest that there are certain *forces* working behind your back. As far as your question is concerned, misdirected or faulty information may sabotage your plans at the present time.

Man/Scythe This is a threatening combination, and therefore, you should act with great caution regarding your question. Elements of jealousy, threats, manipulative maneuvers or even danger may be involved. You may have the sense of someone wishing you ill-will or working to block your efforts and movements. You can be sure that in this situation, whatever opposes you is certainly formidable. Look for things to be torn down or even wiped out, while other areas of your life will be built back up so you can get a new start.

Man/Eye You can expect victory when you hit your target but all may not end pleasantly. Since the central meanings behind these two runes are power and influence, you may soon be meeting up with an individual who influences you heavily—for better or worse. There may be secret dealings where you will be shown something that you have not been aware of before. This will give you a an alternative way out that you hadn't really considered before. All in all, you will become more conscious of your destiny.

Simply put, this combination indicates a powerful figure coming into your life.

HARVEST

Harvest/Crossroads Concerning this matter, you will make substantial progress, but you need to understand this will involve hard work and dedication. You can also expect frustration, but nothing you cannot overcome. In fact, the more you are willing to sacrifice for the greater good, the more you will see many of your goals and dreams realized. Some may experience goals or plans coming to a halt, a standstill, or a face-off. Whatever happens, you will have to remain steadfast and work from a position of strength. It is probably *not* a good time to become lax or permissive with others. Although many of the issues concerning this question will continue to frustrate you, whatever progress you make at this time will be more enduring and substantial than something that comes as a lucky break.

Harvest/Star A good word is coming. Perhaps there will be a decision in your favor. This is an extremely fortunate rune selection; therefore, you can expect to see many of your dreams and visions bear fruit at this time. Some will be awarded payment or compensation, while others will be able to recover favorable opportunities or experiences they may have missed in the past. The star up ahead is a dream coming into fruition. You can expect to be singled out in a most positive way.

Harvest/Waves This combination is also lucky, but with it there are a few warnings. Very shortly, you should be feeling a great deal of optimism. However, you will need to do a reality check on a regular basis. These runes suggest that although your awareness has moved to a higher level, there will be times when your judgment is not good. Therefore, you will tend to paint things the way that you want them to be, not as they really are. In this respect, you could sabotage your own hard work because you refuse to see the real truth. This truth involves change on your part, which is always difficult. This issue probably has to do with the foundation upon which you have built your entire life. At any rate, your random selection is still fortunate, just as long as you do not give yourself over to escapist pursuits and wasteful longings.

Harvest/Scythe On a fundamental level, this rune combination foretells an inheritance, since it suggests you will benefit financially and economically through the death of something. However, there are many ways this can come about. One might benefit through a divorce where joint assets are divided. Some may learn they are owed money when there is a shake-up in either the government, joint finances, or a business. You may even receive an unexpected refund. Whatever the reason, you can look forward to financial gain through the dissolving of joint funds. Another meaning behind this selection is that you will embark on a new path where you must leave the old ways behind. You may also link-up with individuals who may go to extremes, so it is important that you move with caution in all of your relationships—especially with persons you do not know very well.

Harvest/Eye You are about to embark on a journey. Some may experience this journey by traveling across country or visiting foreign lands. Others travel inward and feel this movement on some deep soul level. You can look for encounters with people who are quite different from yourself, well-traveled, freewheeling souls who do not conform to the usual rules. You can look for communications that go beyond the boundaries of your state, your country, or even your universe. Concerning your question, now is the time to break free from limitations. In order to achieve what you have in mind, you must be willing to travel and make the appropriate changes. You must explore.

CROSSROADS

Crossroads/Star A beautiful dream is hovering, one you wish upon, like a star. This rune combination implies longing, but also suggests that your recent efforts have somehow been frozen. Although the circumstances of your life may have taken on a static quality, you are still creating a solid base upon which to fashion your dreams. The Crossroads represent hard luck, so you will have to accept some limitations at this time. Concerning this matter, you will need to seek the help of an authority who is old enough or wise enough to play the role of mentor.

Crossroads/Waves Right now, you must be very certain that you have all of the correct information with regard to your question. Any activity, idea, or relationship that is not grounded in fact will probably not endure. Perhaps this has to do with some earth-shaking truth that, for whatever reason, you have denied, against your own best interests. You may experience some feeling of loss at this time, or you may feel that you have been robbed of something essential. It would be best to bide your time before taking any action concerning this matter.

Crossroads/Scythe This combination suggests caution and with it comes a strong warning. Perhaps you've experienced treachery or devious actions on the part of another. You must now be aware of hazards and deceptions. These particular stones suggest a break, a death, a final resolution to the question you are now posing. At this point, it will be difficult for the matter to progress in the way that you had hoped. In fact, there will be a permanent cutoff, some sense of finality that forces you to take the path you've feared for quite a while. In any event, you will be forced to take this path and in the end, you will win.

Crossroads/Eye   Now is the time to pause and reassess. Now is the time to build a strategy, a working plan. If you begin something without a specific idea, it will probably not work out at the present time. However, if you are willing to work diligently, your efforts should show positive results. What these runes really mean is that you have a power behind you right now. It is a feeling that guides you, something that spurs you onward, almost to the point of an obsession. Shortly, you should have several profound experiences that alter the way you see things. You may also meet a strong rival or someone who challenges you in the way that you need to be challenged. Expect unusual, fated events.

STAR

Star/Waves   A dream realized, a fantasy comes true. Your mind is set on lofty plans. Here, the Star represents focus, while Waves suggest ideals. This is what you pine after, but somehow this beautiful ideal has been denied you. It is now time for you to forget about trivial distractions and shoot for the big dream. To do this, you must clarify and work toward nothing else at this time. You will get your wish, as long as you do not waver from your path and as long as you keep your focus clear. The universe cannot grant your wish unless you are specific about what you want. Now is the time to be specific.

Star/Scythe   As you know, the Scythe can represent an enemy, and other kinds of opposing forces, while the Star brings this into focus. For sure, these are interesting times when you experience both bad and good. In one respect, you will be making major progress and gaining power. You will have the energy and foresight to protect your interests. On the other hand, you can expect other forces to gang up on you just as you are about to achieve your objective. You can see the familiar being cleared away from your life, which may be painful. In the long run, this clearing away will give you the freedom or the push to accomplish what you've always wanted.

Star/Eye This is a combination that is a sign of great power and influence. This combination means that you're now at an advantage. You can expect help, blessings, and other substantial gains. Although this sometimes indicates that the subject you're asking about is now only speculation, it implies you've taken the correct action in this matter. Generally, this combination assures that everything should turn out in your favor, but not without risk and not without the possibility of alienating those with fainter visions. Rarely, this rune combination can indicate sudden fame or great social renown. These runes also suggest the crystallization of a dream where you finally understand some greater purpose. Needless to say, you will begin to understand the overall pattern of your fate. You will grow to understand the greater plan.

 WAVES

Waves/Scythe At this time your dreams will carry you, but unfortunately some will have to be stopped or put on hold. Perhaps you've had some unrealistic expectations, or you've overlooked issues that seem to be too painful to deal with now. Some of you may experience a trauma or a jolt that will force you to find other avenues or directions. Others will be forced to evaluate their failures and build a new strategy based upon the cold, hard facts rather than some illusory dream. This combination can mean dreams gone sour, a betrayal, fear of intimacy, and getting to the bottom. In answer to your question, this selection of runes is not all bad. But in order to get what you're after, you'll have to be truthful with others and brutally honest with yourself.

Waves/Eye It is divined. The fates say *it shall be.* This combination implies good fortune—as long as you are a seeker of truth and are willing to share your good fortune with others. As master of your ship, you now have the power to turn the tides in your direction. This means you are responsible not only for yourself but also the others who follow in your direction. The Eye Rune suggests watching, observation, and scrutiny. When this rune turns up, it can mean that you are no longer anonymous in what you have put into action. You will have to take the credit, and also, the blame. A crowd or a group should have something to do with the outcome of this question. Since Waves are the fleeting image and the eye represents a watcher, some of you can expect to have your likenesses caught on film, videotape, or some other kind of moving image. Also, keep in mind that kindred souls will gather for familiar talk. The turning up of these stones foretell a soul mate who, for whatever reason, cannot be with you at this time.

EYE

Eye/Scythe This is an awesome power. Therefore, whatever shape this power takes, including the outcome, depends entirely upon what you make of it. Like dynamite, this power must be handled carefully and with great attention and discretion. This rune combination can suggest obsessions, power struggles, and hidden jealousies. It is important that you not give in to some of these more negative emotions right now. It can mean that you feel as if your boundaries have been invaded or you have somehow been violated. It can indicate you feel intimidated or threatened in some way. This combination can reveal you are the victim of a psychic attack—so, maintain your boundaries and keep your aura strong. More positively, the turning up of the Scythe and Eye Runes spells out that you will get to the bottom soon. You will finally see what has been hidden from your view.

There is an end to this cycle, and with every end, there is a beginning. This is a time for healing, where you get a fresh start and where everything is made anew.

In any event, there are more routine meanings to this very powerful rune combination and they are: the possibility of vandals in your immediate area, property damage, the airing out of secrets, meeting up with a secretive or awkward person, feelings of shyness or feelings of appearing awkward yourself. Some may experience the loneliness of feeling different from others, or having to go it alone. When you learn to rely on your inner resources and not the opinions of others, you will have reached a turning point. Then the solution to your problem will be absolutely clear.

Asking the Ultimate Question: What About Romance?

During any kind of mystical divination or psychic reading, questions concerning romance are, hands down, the ones most frequently asked. Recent oracles and divination sets emphasize spiritual growth while ignoring the fundamental questions involving romance, which is just another form of spirituality.

Romance, in essence, is one of nature's ultimate highs. It involves the commingling of spiritual energies with more base, earthly principles. Romantic love, for most people, can be the closest thing on earth to standing in the presence of the Creator's divine love. It feels good. And like all things that feel good, it can be destructive or addictive. But this isn't the way it is meant to be.

Throughout our lives, romance continues to crop up even when you'd think we'd be too old to care. Yet we do, since mind and heart never lose the ability to dream and desire. Romance promises the ultimate fulfillment, even in cases where it is only imagined and never becomes a reality. We are all changed by love. We can grow spiritually through various types of relationships, but few can transform us as quickly as romantic love.

When asking your Witch's Runes questions concerning romance, it's important to practice some restraint. Practically, you should only consult the runes every three or four days to discover the really important answers. Obsession, of any kind, will only drive away what it is you desire, and if you ask too often, you won't get a clear answer. It takes that long for trends to develop or the outcome to change. So remember. Don't confuse your runes!

For the most part, you should accept the *first answer* your chosen stone gives you. Learn to take it to heart. But for further clarification, it's all right to draw another rune. However, anything more can skew the accuracy of the stones.

Ready to begin?

Take your bag of runes in hand and ponder the question you are wanting to ask. You may want to envision the face of the person you are inquiring about or make some other kind of psychic connection. The moment the face in your mind's eye no longer seems like a frozen image (watch for a change in expression, for the eyes to move, or the sound of words or breathing), you have made your connection. Ask the question concerning your desire aloud. Make your words clear. Now it is time to consult the runes. Reach into the bag and pull out a stone. Look at the symbol and see what images it evokes. Read the following interpretations concerning romance and the answers the runes offer:

Sun The Sun Rune implies an idealist who follows a noble cause. It can also stand for a pushy, overbearing person who won't allow you to be yourself—the kind who will always want you to be a reflection of her or him. This rune says there is only room for one to shine, and this is what you need to remember. Competing against one another could turn up more often than you'd like. At any rate, the outcome here is still mostly positive. The relationship not only seems important, it is vital and necessary at this very moment. Yet your love interest may be difficult to get close to or may shun intimacy in some way. Expect big crowds, changes, and a sudden turn of events. Ego conflicts and power struggles could happen. A lack of intimacy or closeness would be the downfall of this relationship. On the flip side, this could well be one of the most exciting and nourishing unions you've yet experienced. Make it great.

Moon The Moon Rune gives off a soft and mysterious allure. There is a shy, gentle feeling to the relationship at present, or maybe a hesitancy over getting involved. The psychic connection is strong, but you may also find a sense of alienation or estrangement. Rather than falling head-over-heels in love, this is more gradual. You may sense your lover is holding back or is not committing in the way you'd like. Maybe you get a bit "woozy" or fuzzy-brained over this compelling love interest. Or maybe you just don't know where you stand. Yet this is a person you can share vibes with, the kind who grows on you—like the waxing promise of the moon. It may seem more like a buddy-buddy or good pal kind of thing. Sharing similar dreams and attitudes keeps the attraction at the forefront of your thoughts. This connection will remain markedly important, since it's somehow wrapped up in your fantasy life. Go slow and let things flow.

Flight There is much talk. Any type of communication involving speech or the written word will bring fortunate results. Messages come your way. Important words are spoken and intentions are made clear. Look for phone calls, letters, messages, or faxes giving you the news. Expect plans to be made from afar. Traveling or covering some distance may be involved. In cases of estrangement or separation, a reunion is likely. Much to your surprise, an old lover may contact you or turn up at an unexpected place. You may get surprising proposals or a profession of love. Contacts of all sorts are important now. Ideas are carried, hearts sprout wings and soar. You'll not be grounded in the mundane much longer. You'll hear word soon.

Rings   Choosing the Rings indicates a serious turn to a romantic relationship. On a practical level, the ring represents a marriage of sorts. on a spiritual level, it is symbolic of the binding of two souls. This rune can be one of soul mates or various karmic unions. Most of the time, it indicates a loving partnership or two souls who are well-suited to each other. Sometimes it can mean that you're obsessed with the idea of having a lover. So, watch out for that. You may find that the life of your love interest runs parallel to yours, where personal histories are filled with amazing similarities and weird correspondences. This is an emotional bond not to be taken lightly. Your heart's desire is someone you can't seem to get away from, most likely because you don't really want to.

Romance   This stone could just as well be called Eros, but that would trivialize the gentle play and the sense of childlike whimsy in initial attractions and following romance. On the other hand, the Romance Rune speaks of a magnetic pull, much of it based upon raw animal magnetism. More than any other, the Romance Rune represents *passion, sex,* and *drama*—the highly charged, unforgettable kind. When choosing the Romance Rune, you can figure your attraction is wired with all manner of karma, physical attraction, and an affinity of souls. The only bad thing would be that this kind of attachment can be potentially unhealthy, or in rare instances, it is fraught with danger. This may be a once-in-a-life-time love affair, but too filled with conflict and opposition to be a permanent one.

Woman   Here, there is a changing, shifting feeling to the relationship which, at present, has no real focus. It may be that you sense the romance is not progressing, or somehow your love is unrequited. Communication has stopped. There is distance between you. This stone denotes a parting of ways, although it is probably not final. If you're a woman choosing

this stone, then your lover may be viewing you primarily as a per-
sonification of the feminine (sometimes as an exciting sex object,
or as a dependable mother figure). If you're a man choosing this
stone, your lover may view you simply as a companion or a
friend. In essence, the answer to your question remains muddled
or open-ended. For further clarification, you may want to draw
another rune.

Man   You can also call this rune chaos since it has powerful and disruptive energies. As far as your love life is
concerned, expect things to get stirred up. You probably
won't know what's happening. Don't expect to for a while. You
might say this one foretells a match that can lift you high into the
heavens or send you on a descent into hell. The attraction is immediate, compelling, and deep. It's an either/or situation. Yes, your
must-have-amour has the potential for that kind of intensity. But
it's possible this relationship is one-sided. Most obsessions are.
You'll fight a lot, then end up in bed. Or your lover will make you
miserable over various cat-and-mouse games that tend to trip your
trigger or send you screaming for the funny farm. When the going
gets rough the tough get going. So get ready, love slaves. Prepare for
a bumpy ride!

Harvest   Almost no one thinks of practical angles when
in the grips of lurid love, but now may be the time for
you to consider them. Drawing the Harvest Rune
implies benefits for both, most specifically financial ones. For
instance, issues that involve security (where you're going to sleep
next, hide your broom, or hang your cloak). Sometimes the Harvest
stone can mean that as a couple, the two of you will grow together
through each experience, gradually accumulating knowledge,
wealth, power—whatever values you both agree are important. In
other cases, the balance may not be so equal. One partner will have
more wealth or influence than the other, either by age or social

standing. At any rate, the Harvest Rune foretells happier times are drawing near. This could be your lucky year.

Crossroads This stone indicates a turning point. It can also foretell quarrels or fights. If the romance is just getting started, it will probably not last—yet both parties will end up learning a great deal about the nature of love and also themselves. For long-term relationships, recently unleashed obstacles and complications are now beyond your control. The best advice is to work through the difficulties slowly and make no rash decisions until the quirks can be ironed out. It's possible you're putting up with more than you should. The Crossroads Rune indicates a connection or a bond that is highly karmic, although it may seem to be more like the one bad habit you just can't break. Cultivate patience, Pray like a saint.

Star The Star Rune represents hope and desire. Romantic love has become the thing that you now wish upon—a fixation, if you will. No doubt about it, you find the person in question fascinating, an unusual individual worthy of admiration and worship. Suspended high above, the Star Rune always implies lofty pursuits. In part, this union or romance promises to be ideal, when in reality it may not be able to give you what you need. But you're so enthralled with your lover, you barely notice the pedestal is starting to teeter and sway. The Star Rune symbolizes the need to follow or fixate on an idea or a person, since the star is always up ahead, just above the horizon, out of reach. But don't give up hope. Not at all. The Star Rune makes the promise of wishes fulfilled. If not now, then later. Dream on.

Waves This stone represents fathoms of emotion where love crosses time and distance. You sense you are being carried, swept away by powerful feelings and responses. There is a connection of mind and soul. However, due to outside forces you may be estranged from your heart's desire. The Waves Rune can also represent parting and the shedding of tears. Promises of passion and depth exist here. Bad timing and misunderstandings may have sabotaged the relationship. In rare instances, the Waves Rune can conjure the love of someone you really don't know or have met only briefly. It can mean that you love or pine for someone from afar. It would be wrong to deny the spiritual element to this romance. Your dreams may have led you to this person. This is the one you yearn for, the one who brings your soul peace. Since waves are water, they also suggest reflection. It may be the reflection of *self* that you truly desire. In essence, the message behind the Waves Rune is this: Look to yourself. Cultivate the whole person. Then, after much soul searching, you may look for the other.

Scythe   This is not the most fortunate rune choice, but it does represent a transforming relationship where both are changed dramatically—for better or for worse. The Scythe Rune indicates immediate and compelling attractions—the kind you can't run away from, no matter how hard you try. The object of your desire is unforgettable, overwhelming, and you may feel as if you will go to the ends of the earth to cement the relationship. The problem here is the balance of power where one lover must rule and have dominion over the other. According to the old ways, the Scythe Rune represents parting or a death to the relationship. The romance can have elements of hatred or some deep resentment. At any rate, the scythe is the blade that cuts away, it is the sword of terrible love that binds, blinds, and eventually comes between you. You will find barriers, obstacles, conflicts, and misfortune. This is not so much a romance as it is an entanglement—a passionate and richly imagined obsession. You may want to shop around a little longer before committing yourself to this one.

Eye You have selected the most powerful stone of all, since the Eye Rune represents *you*, and therein lies the rub. More than any other stone, the Eye Rune foretells of the "twin flame," the rarest of all soul mates, coming into your life in one guise or another. In this respect, your mutual attraction or romance is destined in some divine and undeniable way, yet these kinds of bonds are rarely consummated. But this does not mean the relationship will not develop into something more permanent or even that it should not happen. It only means that within a short time, you will know who your twin soul is, what your purpose is in advancing the relationship, and during this time, you will begin to understand your own purpose in a larger and richer way than you ever have before. You will sense that this is a relationship of absolute equality, and although it may have problems, it will not have the types of misunderstandings that most relationships suffer from. Instead, your relationship could suffer because you are too much alike, or the chemistry may not be exactly right, since it does not have the kind of tension that produces sexual passion in any predictable way. This is because relationships between twin souls are not based upon sex, since spirits do not need to recreate themselves, as they are absolute, eternal, and advanced beyond gender. Instead, this bond will have the kind of depth you'll probably never experience with another again, and for that reason, the choice of this stone can indicate that you are entering one of the most exciting and transforming times of your life.

Zodiac of Destiny Reading Method

From the very beginning, human beings have pondered the skies. It was only natural for us to draw parallels and see more than coincidence between what was happening on earth and what was happening with the stars. This speculation eventually led to the oldest science in the world: astrology.

Since astrology is a universal and long-honored tradition, its symbols and motifs are brilliant and awe-inspiring. Like he stars, they seem to speak to our inner cores. One of the most powerful symbols is the astrological wheel that opens up the heavens, enabling us to understand what is happening on earth, not only in the here and now, but also in the future.

Witches have always been practitioners of astrology, reading its signs and tokens, divining and interpreting the movements of the stars. Somehow we have always known that to be close to the sky means to be close to the realm of the spirit.

One way to read the Witch's Runes is to use the Zodiac of Destiny Reading Method. This method will enable you to do a longer reading of the runes with greater variation in their meanings. You may have a certain question in mind or you can do a complete reading by utilizing the horoscope diagram.

Use this method step-by-step as if you are reading a horoscope. If you feel uncomfortable because your knowledge of astrology is limited, you can do the Zodiac of Destiny Reading Method by asking your question and focusing on the runes which fall in the 1st, 4th, 7th and 10th houses.

Ponder their meanings, then read the remaining Witch's Runes and their houses. Look up the explanations of your runes and the astrological houses where they fall. Keep doing this until you get a clear picture concerning the influences that surround your question. Or you can interpret the way the stones fall, for a full reading. But first you must consult your bag of runes.

First, take the Eye Rune out of the bag and place it at the center of the zodiac wheel. In this way, the Eye Rune becomes the matrix, the power point of your reading. You may refer to the Eye Rune several times during the reading for reflection, concentration, and to recharge your energies.

After a brief moment of meditation and centering yourself, begin to pull stones out of the bag. Your first selection will go on the cusp of the First House, your second selection on the cusp of Second House, and so on. Continue selecting stones at random until you finish the twelve points of the wheel when all of your Witch's Runes will be in place for the Zodiac of Destiny Reading Method.

After you have finished selecting your stones, your wheel should look something like the picture on page 152.

Astrology provides the Witch's Runes the planetary correspondences that can be used as keys to unlock the secrets of the horoscope wheel. You can use this reading method if you have no expertise in astrology. However, any knowledge of the zodiac will make the reading easier and more precise.

What Rules Each Rune?

Some of the rune-planet correspondences, such as the Sun and Moon Runes, are more obvious than others and will speak for

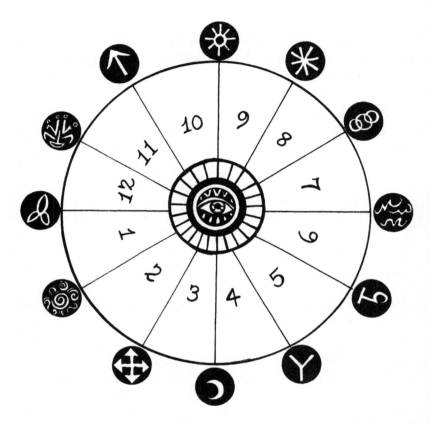

themselves. At any rate, the following keys will help you interpret the meanings behind the runes as they fall in the astrological houses.

Sun Rune is ruled, naturally, by the Sun. This rune sheds light on the issue, clarifying things and bringing them sharply into focus. The Sun also points out power places in your reading. Thus, where the Sun turns up, you can expect much activity or strength. You can be certain that the ego is somehow involved when this stone makes an appearance. The Sun also represents going public, sudden attention, special merit and awards, entertainment, glorious achievement, or fame. You can also be certain that the astrological house this rune falls in is a special point of interest. The meanings behind the house position and rune should be read together. All in all, the Sun Rune is always positive.

Moon Rune is ruled by the Moon. Wherever this stone appears, you can be certain that the question you are posing is somehow linked to your past, especially subjects involving childhood issues. The Moon Rune rules genetics, family, memory, feeling, intuition, instincts, and dreams. This stone stands for inheritances, female relatives, a woman or a man of wisdom. It represents all issues that deal with your past, your history. The moon also suggests the fertile ground of the imagination, states of reverie, surging crowds, trance states, self-preservation, madness, and the public. This rune is enormously magnetic and thus, mostly fortunate.

Flight Rune is ruled by Mercury, and like the planet Mercury the meanings behind this stone involve the news, travel, and all types of communications. Look to the house position where the rune falls. You can expect quick developments in this area, and you can look forward to hearing news about this matter shortly. Issues involving anything that pertains to spreading news, such as television, computers, faxes, or e-mail, will be relevant in this matter. Expect speedy messages which change your course of action, and receiving a piece of news.

Rings Rune is ruled by Venus, which represent partnerships, good vibes, good fortune, easy flow, the appetite, beauty, art, marriage, not wanting to go it alone, and acquired wealth. This rune corresponds to the astrological sign Libra, and thus, it is most fortunate when falling in the Second, Seventh and Eighth Houses. Where the Rings Rune appears, you can look forward to the cementing of important bonds, or even getting a contract or lucky deal having to do with the matter in question.

Romance Rune is ruled by the conflicting energies of Venus and Mars, therefore this stone carries a great deal of weight in any reading, since it has to do with reconciling opposites. You can expect magnetic attractions, romantic estrangement, as well as other intrigues and scandals. With regard to the question you are posing, you can look for open competition, rivals turning up (who are serious about going after what you have!) and emotional maneuvering. You can be assured that the matter pertaining to your question has a great deal of force behind it. You can also expect controversy about this matter.

Woman Rune is also ruled by Venus, but it corresponds more to the energies of the signs Taurus and Cancer. Read this stone first as a woman and pay close attention to what house it falls in. Look at the runes which surround the Woman Rune. Does the Scythe fall near? This could be the ending of a relationship. Is the Eye Rune close by? This suggests psychic development, a strong emotional bond or being watched by another with romantic intentions. This rune can also represent the home and domestic issues and ways of personal enhancement, especially those that relate to your appearance and the way you present yourself. It also has to do with what you personally own. This is a positive rune for business deals as well. For women, this rune represents you in the reading.

Man Rune is ruled by Mars, and thus, the house in which this rune appears will be a place of much physical activity. In general, the Man Rune quickens or speeds up certain actions and developments in the chart. But it is also the rune of recklessness, impulsivity, and certain dangers. You can look for great energy and enthusiasm regarding your project when this stone turns up. You can expect to be forced to assert your position and make your motives known, so this is not a good time to retreat or back down. Therefore, a word of caution is advised for the house the Man Rune falls in. For men, this rune can represent you in the reading.

Harvest Rune is ruled by Jupiter, planet of openness and ease. This stone speaks of obstacles being lifted and important goals achieved, so it is one of the more fortunate runes in the reading. In this way, the Harvest Rune is the payoff for the many projects you have put into action, especially in the areas of interest where you have concentrated most of your energies. Meanings behind the Harvest Rune are abundance, gifts, awards, rewards, travels involving pleasure, and spirituality and the higher mind. Because this rune is even more positive than the Sun, you can expect these issues to be underscored, since the Harvest Rune is essentially the highlight of your reading.

Crossroads Rune Although the message this rune carries can be ominous and it gives a strong warning, there are houses in which the Crossroads Rune falls that are positive in the sense that they represent substantial progress being made (albeit, this progress is slow and you may encounter many pitfalls). If the Crossroads Rune falls in the Tenth House of worldly achievement, in the Sixth House of work, and *sometimes* in the Second House of money, you can expect to make practical or pragmatic progress, specifically in those areas. The energies of this stone correspond to Saturn—planet of hard luck and blocks, but also getting what is due to you. For better or worse, you will soon know the truth. If the energy you put forth is genuine, and you are willing to work hard, you will eventually achieve your objective and your goals. Nothing will be able to stop you.

Star Rune is jointly governed by the planets Uranus and Venus. Therefore, the Star Rune rules your highest goals and dreams, especially those that have impacted your life in a deep or meaningful way. The Star Rune can indicate fame or accumulating property and wealth. The Star implies a precious moment, such as an engagement or a debut, and your place in the spotlight. It speaks of a time when you will get credit for what you do, and you will be rewarded according to the energy you have invested. This stone represents the shimmering veil of the psychic world, since it suggests dreams, hopes, aspirations and visions. The Star Rune can signify money or jewelry, a gift that is richly deserved, based upon diligence and hard work. The Star Rune is symbolic of your most meaningful goals and your loftiest dreams. Look to the astrological house where the Star Rune falls to discover how you can make that dream come true.

Waves Rune is ruled by watery Neptune, planet of deception and unrealized goals. The reading of this stone has a lot to do with what kind of person you are. If you are involved in the arts or spiritual growth, usually this stone is highly positive, bringing in the kind of loftier influences that the creative or spiritual individual needs. However, there are times when the rays of illusion or deception can be especially negative. Thus, these tend to be the areas by which we fool ourselves, such as in our key relationships—governed by the Seventh House; our friendships—governed by the Eleventh House; our children— governed by the Fourth or Fifth houses; and even the First House, which is your very essence, your very self. The Waves Rune also stands for travel, a parting of the ways, music, magic, poetry, art, ill-health, and self-sabotage. Carefully read the house position in which this stone falls for further insight.

Scythe Rune, ruled by Pluto, is the planet of "the hidden," but it is also an avenger and exposer of core truths. Therefore, this is not a very fortunate rune for those involved in denial. The Scythe, like Pluto, can move like an earthquake through the reading, tearing down that which has outlived its purpose, all the while leaving just enough space to build anew. Thus, this stone represents endings: the tearing down or wiping out, but also the building back up. This is especially true of the planet Pluto, which has something to do with actual earthquakes. The Scythe always carries a word of caution when it appears in a reading, as if to say, All things must pass away. But those who accept change have nothing to fear.

 Eye Rune is governed by the Sun and Pluto, both planets of tremendous pull and magnetism. Wherever this stone appears is often an issue of immediate concern and should be addressed accordingly. When the Eye Rune turns up, it has much to do with your reputation and how peers or society see you presently. The mundane meanings behind this rune are cameras, secrets, scandals, psychic powers, and public attention. It also has to do with the meeting up with soul mates, karmic circumstances, and all things of a mysterious nature. The Eye Rune can stand for the witness to the event—one who watches and takes in the information, but does not speak. So be cautious here.

The Astrological Houses

What is of critical importance to the Zodiac of Destiny Reading Method is the symbols behind the astrological houses. In order to understand the meanings behind the stones for this method, you need to also understand the archetypes of the astrological houses. The following are basic meanings behind them:

First House is the Self, the person involved, the central issue, the matter in question and the surrounding circumstances, what has already passed, or that which is already known. This astrological house foretells how you will assert your position, or your self, and what will be involved when you do. The First House represents the body and the appearance, as well as how we view our world. For instance, the Moon or the Scythe Rune would represent dramatic changes or turnarounds in those areas.

Second House reveals what has been purchased, bought, or owned. This includes all manner of finances, assets, possessions, and wealth. In this way, the Second House represents the material world, the world of the earth, and all physical matter. Therefore, this house should be considered when questions of business legalities or finance are involved. It is also an important area in both marriages, joint interests, and partnerships. If your question involves either money, business, or material gain, you will want to pay special attention to the rune that falls in this house.

Third House indicates the message or the communications involved. Third House issues have to do with the way we express ourselves, and what is expressed to us. This house has to do with siblings and the immediate neighborhood. It can also hint at the message we are about to be given, a verdict rendered, and what we choose to do with the information. The Third House points to the truth of certain matters or at the ways that we may choose to delude ourselves or pretend. The particular rune that falls in this house can reveal what people are discussing at present. A contract or agreement is possible now. Listen carefully before you speak.

Fourth House suggests not only the current home but also issues stemming from the early home of our childhood, bad habits that need to be overcome, and ways that we may sabotage our own interests by playing it safe. The Fourth House points out the root cause, and also the ways that we may resist change necessary for growth—including emotional, material, and spiritual aspects. The Fourth House is our collective memory, our history, the group soul, and also the tribe with which we identify. Circumstances involved in the matter of your concern may be traced back to the rune that turns up in the Fourth House. Other issues of the Fourth House include family, tradition, our comfort zone, our emotions, and the imagination.

Fifth House implies all things that bring us pleasure, including playacting, romance, and creativity, as well as our own personal sense of whimsy and play. Subjects that belong to the Fifth House are: drama, art, theater, movies, the stage, ways in which we express ourselves, the public-at-large, the public-as-audience, big plans, television, playgrounds, schools, and amusement parks. The Fifth House can also be the house of childhood after the baby takes her first steps, when she becomes a personality with some sense of mastery over her immediate world. However, the Fifth House is usually looked to as the house of romance and all the pleasures love brings—especially when the romance is in its first stages of blossoming, innocence, and openness.

Sixth House points to our work and the daily routine, the place where most of us spend our hours between nine and five. The Sixth House has much to do with the way we organize ourselves and our lives, and what work must be involved to achieve what we are after. The Sixth House is the house of schedules, organization, debts, and making plans. This can include buildings that work on a schedule, such as a hospital, a library, or a plant with shift work. The Sixth House suggests the time we spend to get the job done. It also brings up certain health concerns. If you have questions concerning health, you will need to pay special attention to the rune that turns up in the Sixth House.

Seventh House speaks of working together as a unit or a team. This may be why the Seventh House is called the House of Marriage, since it has much to do with partners and aligning our energies with another toward one collective goal. While the First House is the Self, the Seventh House is everyone else. This house deals with contracts, agreements, legal affairs, team efforts, property you share with someone else, and various kinds of joint ventures. Marriage, as well as the dissolution of marriages, should be considered when reading this position. The Seventh House points to social affairs, manners, agreements, and seeking approval from the outside world.

Eighth House represents all things basic or hidden and dealings that are not really talked about. This involves taboo subject matter such as death, sex, the occult, and the psychic world of ghosts and spirits. The Eighth House is the bottom line and points to the real issue, rather than the trivial or superficial. For this reason, it is an especially important house in the symbology of the horoscope map and should be looked upon as such. The Eighth House is also considered the House of Karma, since it has to do with the Scorpionic drive to get even or seek revenge. What this really means is that you will get what you have worked for—or perhaps, you will get what you deserve—nothing more, nothing less. One fundamental meaning behind the Eighth House is the death of things, the parting of ways, and endings. Therefore, you can look to the Eighth House and its rune to see how the matter of your concern will end, or at least be resolved.

Ninth House is the place where your world opens up, bringing new challenges and experiences—much of which has to do with embracing new experiences and traveling outside of your immediate world. The Ninth House is the House of the Higher Mind that involves not only areas of learning, but also the religious structure upon which we hang many our beliefs or ideals. The Ninth House is the house of travel, publishing, libraries, and games. It is also the area where we test not only our limitations, but also our freedom. In this way, we must move outside the comfortable worlds of our homes and groups of friends to meet larger challenges and bigger issues. The Ninth House is the house of exploration, testing limits, journeys, and foreign lands.

Tenth House is the House of Success and Accomplishment. The rune that falls here suggests the outcome of your question and its ultimate fulfillment—especially that which has to do with prestige, social status, or reputation. The Tenth House shows how you appear before the world (at least the world which you deem important) as well as how successful the end result of your energies and efforts will be. Such rewards usually only come about after some long and deliberate effort, creating results of true substance. The Tenth House suggests your standing in the world and long-term goals rather than any fly-by-night stroke of good luck. Things do not come easily through the struggles of the Tenth House, but what is won is usually quite enduring. This house also has to do with age and aging. It can indicate dealings with older people, the elderly, or those in authority. Turn to this part of the chart for special wisdom.

Eleventh House suggests our hopes, wishes, and aspirations—especially in the way that we relate to our peer group. This house represents clubs, friends, professional organizations, and ideals. By this, we mean the world of cliques and people already friendly to us, and with each other. Through the Eleventh House, we meet like-minded people and thus, we feel less lonely on this lonely planet. We turn to the Eleventh House for speculation, for friendly alliances, and for reading oncoming trends and developments. You can look to the rune in this position to see how well the substance of your question will be accepted or perceived by others, especially those who seem to be part of the group with which you identify. The Eleventh House is also the house of the new and untried. It has much to do with taking risks and what lies outside your current field of vision. It is outer *and* inner space, *and beyond.*

Twelfth House is concerned with the realm of spirit and deals with how you isolate yourself from others. In this way, Twelfth House matters have to do with you as a solitary seeker, where nothing can stand between you and your creator, as well as with the cosmos. The Twelfth House indicates what it is you have to give, selflessly, and for a cause greater than your own ego or personal needs. Some have referred to the Twelfth House as "the unlived life," but really its concerns have more to do with larger issues than selfish gain. For this house, you must look to the way you sabotage yourself and your own interests, and also why. Is your life a self-imposed prison or simply a little piece of heaven on earth? The Twelfth House has everything to do with hospitals, prisons, and institutions where people are put away so they can no longer be seen and are avoided. Thus, this position can let you know what you might be avoiding.

Using the principles of astrology is just another way of reading the Witch's Runes. If you're involved in other forms of divination, such as tarot cards or tree oracles, you can easily adapt those techniques when reading your magick stones.

Don't be afraid to use your creativity and talents to develop unique reading methods. Like the runes, creative ideas are free-flowing and adaptable. Drawing upon your creativity and intuition can only enrich your methods of rune casting. The more you flow with your hunches, the better your psychic reading will be. The sky is the limit!

PART 5

Spells and
Blessings

itches have always been associated with magick spells. At their worst, they've been said to hex and give curses, too. But did you know that witches also impart blessings?

Many of the faery tales we have been brought up on involve the idea of witches and faeries casting spells, cursing, and granting wishes.

Why cast spells? There is a long history of spells in witchcraft, as well as many taboos. After all, if a witch can cast a spell for good, can't she also condemn with her powers?

Of course she can. But most don't.

It is not her wish to spread negativity, for the witch knows whatever she sends out comes back tenfold.

The use of spells is very practical. Spells can save time by lifting obstacles, can set an event or a goal into action, and can be used to stop evil. Blessings can bring on good fortune or set the wheels into motion for a wished-for goal or event. Blessings can bring peace, harmony, and balance to your life.

The following are some suggestions on how to cast spells by using a few simple exercises along with your runes. Take heed and use caution while you're still learning. Wish for good and banish bad. In the meantime, happy casting!

Using your Powers

We have more influence over how we live than we are led to believe. In recent years, it has become abundantly apparent that something as simple as a thought can affect the outcome of our lives.

Most of us fulfill the prophecy of what we've been told as children, whether we like it or not. This can be dangerous if as children we only encounter depressing, ignorant people with nothing but negative thoughts. This is why it's so important to hold strong convictions that are positive, but even more important, thoughts that are generous and life-affirming.

Thoughts can shape the reality of our future, but it's important to keep in mind that a positive thought alone cannot stop a bullet speeding toward you. (That is a physical action, while thought is a psychic action.) One thought cannot turn back a hurricane. A positive thought cannot bring back the dead—at least not in any physical way. Thinking optimistically cannot stop life changes that are inevitable and simply a part of the nature.

Witches realize it is nature, both earthly and cosmic, that dominates the quality of our lives. Witches also know that nature is cyclical, where there is a continuance and nothing is ever lost. What goes away always comes back—although not necessarily in the same form.

Witches can intuit the rhythms of nature, learning how to bend with them like the willow tree. When the stars are just right, when the collective energies are the most sharp, witches can bend the powers that be to *their wills* simply by using the powers of their minds, often with the assistance of elementals, guides, and other helper divinities.

Strangely, most religions seem to miss our connection with nature and its cycles. At a core level, many contemporary religions believe we die, we menstruate, we have labor pains, live poor, go hungry, sicken, and die because we or our ancestors have somehow been bad. We are punished for following our instincts. These ideas seem primitive, yet they are still with us.

Some believe that to follow our own true natures is to directly rebel against our Creator, or God. As they see it, God is in the sky and we are on earth. As long as we are on earth, we cannot be intimate with anything spiritual. As humans, we are debased and limited by Mother Nature, which is ungodly. We are victims of fate. We are earthbound.

Yet the earth is filled with mystery, magic, and various spiritual nuances. If we choose, we can learn to use these forces not only for our material benefit, but also for spiritual growth. Witches understand it is not wrong to be human or to be in tune with nature and her nurturing energies and magickal expressions. It is not wrong to use these spiritual forces, which tend to be neutral, to improve the circumstances of our lives, as well as the lives of others.

The Need for Spells

Are spells the result of aligning with dark forces, as some believe? The answer is no. When people have low or evil impulses, they are usually not spiritual and are lacking in spiritual powers. Being base or greedy is the opposite of being spiritual. Sometimes evil people can hold sway over others, but this is usually a result of their manipulative personalities, not their psychic powers.

Of course there are rare exceptions of people who have developed psychic ability and have then decided to use it in an evil or misguided way. But to be a good psychic, a good witch for that matter, you must be strongly empathetic. After all, being empathetic is what being psychic really is! Therefore, when the person decides to use this ability for his or her own evil purposes, it's usually taken away just as quickly. They start to lose their accuracy as psychics and, eventually, their credibility.

Precisely, what is a spell? A spell is like a wish, but with more power and conviction behind it. A spell is what dreams are made of. You turn your mind and heart in a certain direction, and eventually, reality takes on the shape of what you wish or desire. In this way, destiny is fulfilled when obstacles are lifted. Certain rituals and tools, such as the Witch's Runes, can help you focus your energies when it comes to casting spells and making them work.

In recent years, those who write popular books about keys to success have written about the importance of having a clear vision about what we want out of life. Those who have something specific in mind have far greater luck in getting what they're after. People with muddled visions usually have difficulty getting things to work out, since they aren't sure what it is they really want out of life.

When we think of the spell as a profoundly focused thought, this takes the mystery out of it. In fact, those who are spiritually gifted from birth—some may even think of these souls as witches—rarely, if ever, cast a spell. Such people have a clear vision, a sense of flow, and good intuition. Therefore, they tend to avoid major stumbling blocks. In fact, psychic ability and spiritual powers can be simply described as having an unusual amount of wisdom and good instincts.

But there are times when spells are necessary. Often we face powerful obstacles in our lives that have nothing to do with how hard we've worked or how disciplined and loving we are. There are times when we just get lost in the shuffle, or other forces are at work trying to defeat our goals.

In the modern world, it's not uncommon for many people to be after the same goal. We live in a highly competitive society. You have probably noticed that those with the loudest voices often end up with the grandest prizes, leaving out those whose hearts and intentions are the most gentle and dignified.

So what are some circumstances that cry out for magickal help?

Emergencies, of course, that involve your well-being or that of others are always a top priority. Spells to assist the weak, innocent, and downtrodden are also important. Healings are also essential.

What about spells that help you win over others? Are these ethical? Rarely. For this, you must carefully weigh and consider your own motivations. Are your motives self-serving? Are you trying to defeat individuals who are as worthy of a goal as you are? If your answer is no, then proceed with your spell. In general, it's best to cast a spell that will work to enhance your luck and your chances, rather than relying on a spell to defeat someone else. In fact, if you feel you have an enemy or some opposition undermining your success, it's best *not* to concentrate on that person or group. You will only be reinforcing the bond. Instead, you should focus on improving your lot without intervening in someone else's destiny. Let nature take its course. Their luck, after all, is between them, their gods, and the stars. You have nothing to do with the matter.

In general, all spells that involve negatives are poor reasons to cast a spell, and therefore, they are unethical. Be wary of defeating someone else for your own selfish purposes, gaining power just for the sake of having power, wishing bad luck on others, following frivolous pursuits and selfish goals, winning at love just to play around, attracting negative entities or malevolent spirits to carry out evil wishes, or attracting money or possessions when you have no real need for them.

Here are some good reasons to cast a spell or invoke a blessing.

- For protection, *period.* (It doesn't matter who it is, as long as the person isn't a sociopathic dictator, a child molester, or a serial killer. Almost everyone is worthy of protection—barring a few human monsters who only use their powers to destroy.)

- To turn your luck around.
- To heal someone of an illness.
- To cleanse and purify sacred areas, as well as your home.
- To enhance your finances when you are down on your luck.
- To bring warmth and food.
- To complete an important goal, one you are serious about.
- To find peace of mind.
- To protect you from those who wish to harm you.
- To repel any negativity that comes your way.
- To enhance awareness or creativity.
- To improve health and stamina.
- To get in touch with higher beings.
- To get in touch with your higher self.
- To communicate with nature spirits and elementals.
- To communicate with angels.
- To help you gain wisdom.
- To bless a gathering of kindred souls.
- To insure a safe trip.
- To gain mastery over your immediate world.
- To fulfill something that you know to be destined or a correct course of action.

Spells and blessings follow that you may want to use. After getting used to them, feel free to create some of your own.

house Blessing

Houses hold in and also radiate energies both positive and negative. This fact is obvious even to people who have no mystical gifts whatsoever. We've each heard our share of ghost stories about haunted houses. This makes sense, since human beings generally make love, fight, throw parties, laugh, play jokes, sicken, and die—away from the prying eyes of others, often inside their own homes. This is a lot of emotional baggage for houses to carry. These past energies and vibrations eventually wash over those who currently live inside.

It's no surprise that houses, most especially older homes, can be real psychic hot spots. Houses, like everything else, absorb vibrations. In fact, events that have gone on inside the home can actually become a part of the house's structure. Drive down any neighborhood and you will notice the careworn faces of some older homes, while others appear cheerful and filled with light. Sometimes these vibrations are not always welcome, especially when you're trying to live in peace while ghosts and mischievous spirits emanating from the past have decided to crash your home and move right in.

I grew up in a haunted house (I guess that explains why I turned out the way I did). Although the experience was richly fascinating, the presence of spirits got to be a nuisance. It was hard to sleep through all of the rappings and bangings and weird music that went on all night long. My sister and I finally got wise to our ghost. After he'd start his rapping act (I use "he" most generically) I would clear my throat and calmly call out, "Mother, he's doing it again." My mother would get up and swing through our room, looking under the bed, checking the closets, then the windows. Afterward, my mother would say aloud, "I don't want any more noise tonight!" and then she would slam the closet door shut with a BANG! That would calm the spirits down. At least, until the next night.

Ghosts are amazingly obedient to authority. In general spirits tend to gravitate toward children because they are open and have not built the psychic defenses around themselves, as many adults have. Psychics also attract ghosts because they, like most children, are open. Often people living in haunted houses are psychic. The ghosts draw upon this psychic energy to make an appearance. But many apparitions that appear in haunted houses are "recordings," a residual energy that lives on after the person has died.

These apparitions, or recordings, are much like a videotape of an event which, through some intense emotion or trauma, has somehow imprinted on space and time. How this is done is not really understood. But spirit recordings and apparitions are the most common form of ghost.

Many credible ghost sightings have been reported on Civil War battlefields in the southeastern United States, where entire companies of men are reportedly seen. This falls under the category of ghostly recordings, which often repeat the same activity, over and over again. Recordings are harmless ghosts but impossible to communicate with.

There are also negative entities, which are malevolent ghosts, but they are rare. With everything in life, there is an opposite or opposing force; thus, there are evil spirits that enjoy tricking and debasing humans, especially those on a spiritual path. Probably this is the reason most religions discourage contacting spirits just for fun. For the most part, this is a valid suggestion.

Cleansing Your Home of Unwanted Spirits

To drive away unwanted spirits, and to cleanse your home of negative vibrations, there is a ritual using herbs along with the Witch's Runes that is quick and easy to perform.

At your favorite health or metaphysical shop, buy some sage, cedar chips, sweetgrass, or your favorite sweet-smelling incense. You'll also need some bird feathers or a fan. You can create your own fan by folding heavy paper, but be *very* careful—we don't want your house to burn down before you get a chance to bless it! Sprinkle some of the herbs into the bottom of a ceramic bowl or *clean* metal can. You will want to make a facsimile of the following runes:

EYE	STAR	MOON	SUN

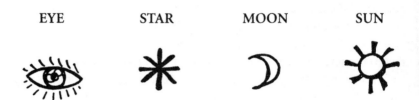

After you have created your own runes (don't worry if the symbols turn out a bit crude; after all, *they are powerful—they are yours!*), you will want to determine the location of the four directions in your home. (You can get a compass if you like, but sunrise and sunset should give you a pretty accurate idea of where east, west, north, and south are situated.)

Place the four runes in a left pocket—the nearer to your heart, the better. Carefully, start burning your sage or incense. As the sage begins to smoke, walk toward the north while fanning the smoke before and after you. Ideally, go to a window at the most northern corner of the room. If there's no window go to a table or other surface, and place your stone. Your first stone will be the Eye Rune. As you place the stone toward the north, which is the point of introspection, utter this modest blessing:

Toward northern lights,
I place the Eye
to act as watcher and my guide,
to drive away that which is not mine,
to drive away what I do not claim.
Spirits not invited to my home.
So shall it be!

Next proceed to your southernmost room. For this, use the Star
Rune. Whisper this small blessing:

Toward southern lights,
I place this Star.
to guard my house from near and far
Spirits that play, must go away,
spirits that curse must be dispersed,
by this cleansing light which is a Star.
So shall it be!

Turn east. While still fanning smoke or incense to spiritually cleanse
the floor level of your home, continue with this blessing by using
your version of the Moon Rune:

Toward eastern light,
I place the moon,
night power of the Witch's Rune,
to send your mischief on its way,
to make you flee before the day
to drive you out and very soon.
So shall it be!

To conclude, proceed toward your westernmost room while still
fanning smoke. Pull out the Sun Rune, the brightest star, and place
it in the westernmost corner while saying this blessing:

Toward western light,
I place the Sun,
to drive out bad. To make you run!
For in this house, I am ONE!
You spirits flee—I have WON!
The bad must leave. And it is done.
So shall it be!

The best time to perform this ritual house blessing is during a new moon, when the heavens are dark. The spirits will generally want to flee in that direction, since black absorbs negativity. Wait until the full moon to gather up your stones, as the full moon sheds light on the situation.

Keep in mind that if you are a witch born, the spirits will probably make a comeback in about six weeks, or others will appear to take their place. For those who are psychic, you will probably want to get used to the fact that spirits will always be a part of your life. They are not likely to go away permanently, but you can keep the destructive ones at bay.

Keep your house spiritually monitored. A sudden drop in temperature, repulsive odors, or the appearance of terrifying night visitors can indicate the presence of negative entities.

If all else fails, contact a professional witch or a psychic to do a cleansing ritual. If you don't know of any witch or psychic, contact a member of the clergy. As mentioned previously, these kinds of spirits are usually uncomplicated. They are relatively easy to manipulate and tend to be obedient to any kind of spiritual authority. Remain strong.

Love Spells

Without a doubt love spells are the most popular spells of all, but they can also be the most tricky and unethical. Before you decide to cast a love spell, you need to make sure that you're not trying to influence someone against his or her will. This can never work in any permanent way.

Of course, the argument can be made that all manner of falling in love is basically against our will. After all, who would intentionally seek those bittersweet pangs of romantic agony? Just a few starry-eyed romantics who still believe that the full moon is meant only for them!

The most unethical love spell of all is one where the object of your desire is already attached—to someone else! The same might be said if you are also in a similar state of attachment.

What about when the person is in an unhappy relationship? That is up to you and your conscience to decide. However, it goes without saying that a love relationship has a better chance of surviving if you both start with a clean slate.

In general, love spells are for the young. After you live a while, you learn to attract what you really need. This is based on the fact that many of our most powerful attractions turn out to be ill-fated love affairs. However, if your heart is set on someone who seems too shy or unavailable to come to you through ordinary circumstances, you might want to try a gentle, cosmic shove to get the relationship started.

To begin your spell, you will need a wine-colored candle, since deep red stands for passion. The energy that sexual attraction creates is wildly powerful. If it weren't, life of all kinds would not go on. You will also need a blank piece of paper and a red felt-tip pen. If you know your beloved's birthday or have a piece of their handwriting, all the better. Any of these items indicates that a certain amount of intimacy between you already exists, so the spell has a better chance of working.

You will also need two index cards of any color—I like the really bright ones. Most office supply stores carry a rainbow of colors. I prefer purple (to spiritually bless) or red (to send out the desire in the right directions) or green (to heal and nurture the bond).

For the next step, you will have to rely on your own creativity. Find a photograph, print, or drawing that somehow holds special significance for both you and the object of your desire. For instance, if you met him or her during a rainstorm, find a photo of rain or storm clouds. A picture (that you draw and color yourself) of your beloved or of a red heart would be splendid. If you're estranged from someone you've shared a child with, a photograph of the child would be a reminder of your special bond.

On the rare occasions I cast spells (for the most part, I accept what life offers as a learning experience and see no reason to challenge the overall pattern of my destiny), I use a black-and-white postcard of my patron saint—Edgar Allan Poe! Don't laugh. To me, Poe stands for the mysterious powers of night. His spirit continues to hold allure, and no doubt his influence will spill over even into the next century. At any rate, put these items aside to use later in your spell.

Now it is time for you to pick out the Witch's Runes to help you focus with the right kind of energy. The first stone you need to find is the Eye Rune, to help you connect spiritually. The next stone should be the Romance Rune, to help kindle the desire. You may

hesitate to choose the next stone since it is the Rings Rune, representing wedding rings in the old Gypsy readings and divination sessions. After all, not everyone wants to *marry* the person he or she
is attracted to! You need not worry. The three rings in the shape of
the trinity shows the souls of two people coming together and creating a third, unique "oversoul." On a physical, more mundane
level, the Rings can represent a child in the future. But for now, the
Rings Rune implies a highly spiritual kind of romantic love—and,
hey, who's against that?

The last and fourth stone you choose is the Flight Rune, representing the carrying of the love and intentions of your heart to the
mind of your beloved. The Flight Rune brings the thought of you
into your beloved's awareness, tugging at his heart and soul.

Your next step is to find a quiet place where you will not be
disturbed. After finding your spot, place the four Witch's Runes
in the shape of a diamond. The Flight Rune should be at the top,
the Romance Rune on the bottom, the Eye Rune to the left, and the
Rings Runes to the right.

Mentally, draw a cross between the four corners. At the very center of the cross—where your minds and hearts meet—is where you
should place the red candle. Naturally, you will need a secure can-
dlestick. Also, after lighting your candle, be *extremely* cautious with
all of your paper objects. *Do not* wear anything with long, flowing
sleeves. It's wonderful to be magickal—but not to the degree of
going up in a puff of smoke! Ideally, wear your underwear, and tie
back your hair. This should allow you to safely be in close contact
with the flame.

After you have lit your red candle, you will notice the flame
starting a dance that is synchronized to your own energy and
thought. Fire really is amazing to behold. Spiritually, fire (and also
electricity) is very responsive to a change in vibrations or the emotional tone in the room.

After your fire has stabilized, blur your eyes, and stare at your
candle until you feel a bit woozy. You are now in a light trance state.

It is time to ask for the protection of your guides. Do this before proceeding with your spell.

Think of your lover and feel the spiritual fire moving up from your groin into your solar plexis. Allow yourself to smile and bask in the presence of your love. Let fantasies flourish! Then for a moment, break the light trance and pull out your blank strip of paper. With the felt-tip pen write the name of your beloved seven times *backwards*. (For witches, to speak backwards is a way of reaching him or her on a deep soul level.)

As an example, here is the way you would write the masculine name Steve:

EVETS
EVETS
EVETS
EVETS
EVETS
EVETS
EVETS

Now, you are to repeat your name of choice backwards at least seven times. After doing this, fold your paper into a small square. Place this square in the shape of a diamond and draw a cross representing the crossroads where your loves shall meet, come together, and bear fruition.

If you like, you may draw symbols on your square of paper. Planetary symbols can represent the celestial powers found in this solar system. I prefer the symbol for Pluto, ♇, which represents the powers of attraction, Venus, ♀, which stands for mutual sharing and love, Mars, ♂, for good sex (only if it happens to turn up) and lastly, Jupiter, ♃, to bestow its blessing on the relationship.

For something less complicated, you may want to use the symbol the Gypsies have always preferred in their love rituals and this is the sign of the heart—simple but to the point!

Here is what your square of paper should look like:

Blow out your candle and give thanks to the angelic powers of the four directions, and the elemental powers as well, which have come to aid you in your quest. You will want to continue this same ritual for the next three days, again, in solitude.

During the daylight hours, you will want to wear this square of paper nearest to your heart. While wearing this square, allow yourself to fantasize freely about your love interest. Remember! Thoughts can bend and influence the outcome of your actions in your favor. This is the fundamental rule of spell-casting and witchcraft. If you think it, dream it, and believe it, then you will achieve it.

On the fourth day, you will want to take the square of paper and staple it between the two index cards. Tape your magickal picture, drawing, or emblem to the outside of your cards. Softly kiss the picture, call out for your true love to hear you, and place your card on a shelf surrounded by the things you love. Dried flowers, figurines of birds, miniature paintings, and candles can make a pretty little altar that seems so much a part of your decor that no one is likely to ask questions.

Wait three weeks to allow your love charm to work. If you see no results in that period of time, you can attempt to recast your spell another two or three times. If things still don't work, let it go. This love wasn't meant to be yours.

Spell to Insure Safety

For this spell, you will need a sky-blue candle of any kind. Again you will draw four stones. These are: the Eye Rune (to keep watch over you or your subject); the Flight Rune (to carry your request for protection to the God or Goddess of choice, your angel, or your guides); the Sun Run (to radiate rays of safety your way); and the Moon Rune (to enhance your intuition and help you make the right choices).

Fashion your stones into a diamond shape with the Eye Rune at the top, the Flight Rune at the bottom, the Moon Rune to the left and the Sun Rune to the right. Place your blue candle at the center, again, where the crossroads meet. The crossroads are a place of all magical beginnings!

Light the candle and gaze into the flame. (Go soft focus, if you can.) Imagine your friend, or even yourself, standing before you. In your mind's eye, place your subject in a chrysalis of brilliant, white light. Imagine this robe of white light as powerful spiritual protection that cannot be penetrated by evil or harm.

Softly, speak this blessing:

> Bless this one [name]
> with blessed light,
> keep [name] safe
> through day and night,

angels come, guides make haste,
keep this soul from ruin or waste,
away from harm, injury, fright,
save this child from what isn't right!
So shall it be!

Blow out your candle. Your spell is complete.

Spell to Get Rid
of Someone Troublesome

In general, a compassionate approach toward others is the best way to lead your life. By helping those in need, you are also helping yourself. *This is the golden rule.* However, there are a few exceptions. These exceptions are individuals who do not really want help. Instead, what they *really* want is to sap your vital energy and keep you from doing important things so they can have you all to themselves. These people are often referred to as psychic vampires—the more you give, the more they take. And like the victim of a vampire, if you don't get rid of them, expect to have your life wrecked and your health ruined. Yes, they can be *that dangerous.*

Probably, these are baby souls in the beginning stages of their earthly life, much in need of love and attention. But there comes a time when you must send these baby souls on their way if you are to have any life of your own. By delaying this end, you are not really helping them. In fact, you are impeding their spiritual growth (and yours, as well) by not insisting that these confused and troublesome souls face the consequences of their actions.

People with kind and nurturing personalities are an easy mark for these types. Since tender-hearted, gentle people don't like to see others suffer, these pesky souls will constantly bring up the fact of their suffering, wearing it like a badge. However, you'll soon notice how they refuse to take any responsibility for their suffering. But in order for these souls to mature and grow spiritually, they simply must suffer. (This, undoubtedly, is the second golden rule.) Nothing really worthwhile comes easily. Yet this is the lesson that must be learned before the soul can progress to the next level. Likewise, these souls really cannot be *led* gently in the right direction. They need to be jolted, forced, or shocked into making improvements in themselves and their lives; but most of the time, even this doesn't work.

To make a nuisance go away, you will need to draw these four stones: the Eye Rune will help give you the power and authority to make them leave, the Crossroads Rune should block their entrance to your home, the Moon Rune will summon angelic and elemental forces as protection for your soul, and the Scythe Rune will cut off that which is no longer needed in your life.

A black candle is especially appropriate, since black represents the end to something. However, if black makes you nervous, white should work just as well. After all, it's only the intention that really matters. Take a black or dark blue scarf and place it on your table or altar area. Leave your scarf in the shape of a square. Place the Crossroads Rune in the upper left corner, the Eye Rune goes in the upper right corner, the Moon Rune in the lower left and the Scythe Rune at the lower right edge. Mentally draw an X between all of the corners and their runes and place your candle at dead center where the lines overlap. As you know, where two lines converge, such as the meeting of streams or rivers in nature, there is a power vortex. Hence, you are creating your own charged area. This setup has been found to be extremely powerful, so go gently with this incantation:

> Powers of air, come to me!
> Free me from this misery,
> Friend or foe, pest or guest,
> drive this [woman/man] from my house!

Spirits fly fast, angels make haste,
chase this nuisance from my place!
No longer do I count (name) friend or foe.
Leave my presence. Out you go!
So it shall be!

Your next step is to take your broom or the limb of an oak tree and draw a circle around your home three times. Take your time, since you must invest in this ritual psychically to really make it stick. It's probably best to perform this ritual during a new or full moon, when the lunar forces are especially sharp-edged and pristine.

If you are truly intent about getting rid of this person, act self-involved. People who fall under the category of the psychic vampire are only out for themselves. Sad but true, the less you give psychic vampires, the less reason they will have for coming around to take from you or disrupt your life. It isn't worth sacrificing yourself and your own peace of mind to keep from hurting such a person whose main intent is to use you.

Therefore, keep the Spell to Get Rid of Someone Troublesome in mind. It would be wise to continue drawing with your broom your magick witch circle around your home at the time of either the full or new moon. This will keep all kinds of negative influences away.

According to old European legend, vampires cannot come into your home (or your life) unless you first invite them in. Remember this the next time you feel your energy waning!

TREE BLESSING

Witches and trees have always been intimate friends. After all, trees are sources of great energy and healing power. Trees are the silent watchers that soak up vibrations from all manner of life, both in heaven and on earth. Perhaps this is because the branches of trees seem to extend into the skies while their roots brace them against the elements and weather by burrowing deeply into the earth. Human beings stand upright, too, just like trees, leaving our minds to ponder the heavens while our feet are planted firmly on the ground.

Scientists know that trees can provide essential medicines to protect our health and keep our bodies from harm. The bark from the willow tree once provided acetylsalicylic acid that helped make aspirin. The bark from the slippery elm is still used to alleviate and speed up the recovery of laryngitis or a sore throat. Most recently, it has been discovered that the bark from the yew tree, a shrub once planted in cemeteries to drive away evil spirits, is possibly a cure for ovarian cancer (if it is caught in its early stages).

Not only can trees shelter our physical bodies by becoming the wood that creates our homes, trees can also provide protection for our emotional bodies and our aura fields. The auras of human beings tend to waver and change, leaving us open to various kinds of psychic assaults. Negativity can play upon our emotions, our bodies, and defenses like a Faustian violin. The auric field of a tree,

though not as finely tuned as ours, is centered, immensely powerful, and strong. One might call the tree the ox—the beast of bur-
den of the plant world.

Drawing energy and strength from a tree is especially effective
when used as a defense against psychic attack. Hostile vibrations and
negative projections from others can wear down all of our systems.
It is generally accepted that positive thoughts, whether through
prayer, invocation, or group synergy, can affect not only our health
but also the outcomes of our lives. The same might be said of negative energy. Consequently, if you become the focus of hostile energies
over a period of time, you will eventually feel these energies pull at
you and wear you down. Often, the way this first manifests is depres-
sion, fatigue, or as mysterious and unexplained illnesses.

One way to build up your auric field is to join your aura with
that of a favorite tree, preferably one close to your home. It doesn't
matter what kind of tree it is, just as long as the tree is mature and
in good condition. Witches, of course, have favorite trees such as
the oak, the hemlock, the maple, the holly tree, and the sycamore,
but you should choose any tree which strikes your fancy. Pick a
nearby tree in order to have daily access to it. Also, spring, summer,
and fall are the best times for tree rituals, but tree rituals can also
be performed during temperate days in winter.

Remember. The idea is not to impose *your* energy on the tree,
but to allow the tree to impose *her* energy upon you. Think of it
this way: The tree is the mother and you are the child. The tree is
your teacher and you are the student. The tree is your lover and you
are the beloved. The tree is the priest and you are the initiate. Learn
from the tree. She has much to offer.

Before you begin the ritual to ask for a blessing from the tree,
you may want to make copies of the following runes. You can do
this by drawing the rune symbols on flat stones, bits of paper, or
pieces of wood. You can also use stones from your set of runes.
However, many prefer to keep their runes for psychic readings and
their runes for spell-casting separate.

MOON   **SUN**   **STAR**   **WOMAN**

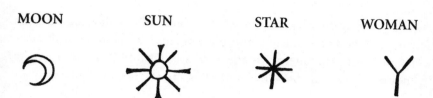

Wait for the next full or new moon. Put the runes in your pocket and go out at dusk when the faery energies are most strong. Before this time, however, you should have already decided upon your tree. Sit down against its base. Close your eyes. Press or roll your spine against the trunk.

Imagine. Dream. Relax. Yawn. Voyage inward.

Surrender to the energy of the tree. Make up a chant. Sing a little song. Connect with the music that resonates through the center of the tree. As soon as you feel yourself becoming completely calm and a part of the twilight energies that surround you, stand up, and begin to place your runes around the base of the tree.

At moon rise, face the east. Place the Moon Rune at the base of the tree. The east is the direction of what has passed and it is also the direction of protection. The shielding energies of the moon work well, since this Gypsy symbol has been known as "arms of protection." Softly repeat this blessing:

> Arms of tree
> protect me.
> I am mine
> and also thine.
> From this eastern direction
> your arms of protection.
> Hold me.
> Shield me.
> Bless me.

The western direction represents the dying of the day, but also the future. Take the Sun Rune and place it close to the base of the tree facing west. The energy of the sun is less subtle than that of the moon. Repeat this blessing:

> Arms of tree,
> direct me.
> I am mine
> and also thine.
> From the western direction
> your rays of protection.
> Hold me.
> Shield me.
> Bless me.

The northern skies signify introspection. They are represented by the Star Rune, which stands in for the north star if not visible on the night of your self-blessing. Place the Star Rune at the northern base of the tree and say this incantation:

> Arms of tree,
> connect me.
> I am mine
> and also thine.
> From the northern direction,
> your winds of introspection.
> Hold me.
> Shield me.
> Bless me.

The southern skies lend power and mystery to any spell or blessing. After all, the south represents unexplored lands and speculation. For this incantation, place the Woman Rune at the southern base of your tree. The Woman stone stands for feminine aspects such as safety, comfort, creativity, the magic wand, but most

important, the branches of a tree. Repeat the following words when
placing your stone:

> Arms of tree
> direct me.
> I am mine
> and also thine.
> From the southern direction
> I ask your protection.
> Hold me.
> Shield me.
> Bless me.

Your next step is to pick up a stick and use it as a source to direct
or receive energy from the tree. In this way, the twig becomes your
magic wand. Walk around the tree from left to right three times.
Lightly touch the base of the trunk as you move in a circular direction. Here is what you should say:

> Mother Tree
> protect me.
> I am mine
> and also thine.
> From all directions
> I seek your protection.
> Hold me.
> Shield me.
> Bless me.

Don't relax just yet for your spell is not complete. You will need to
continue interacting with your tree for at least three weeks. (There
are some who believe you need to continue touching base with
your tree not only for *now* but always.) One good way of staying in

contact with your tree, is to touch or pat it before leaving your home each morning, and also when you return later in the day.

When darkness falls, you may want to slip outside and wrap your arms around the trunk of your tree. It may seem childish to call this a tree hug, but that's what it is. Trees are magnificent presences in our world, not the inert objects that we are led to believe they are. In many ways, trees are more present and belong to this world more than we do. In any event, breathe in the tree's fragrance. Stroke the ripples in her bark. Listen for the weighted throbbing of her wooden heart. Feel the tree energy wiggle beneath your fingers. At this time, you will want to enter into a silent conversation with your tree. Ask for the tree energy to stay with you and guide you during tough times. The power of the tree will not only help strengthen you, she will absorb any negativity that you encounter during the day by sending these toxic thought forms and energies directly into the ground. Trees are terrific transformers of energy, mostly because of their density. They are good at trapping the more base vibrations by keeping them grounded until they are changed or transformed. It is very difficult for these lower vibrations to rise out of the ground. It is more natural for them to sink.

Give thanks to your tree and her friends, the four directions. Whenever you feel your life force or energy waning, you can repeat the tree blessing ritual.

Spell to Attain your heart's Desire

Before attempting this spell, you may want to refer back to page 168 to make sure your sense of ethics and integrity is in good order. It is never wise to cast a spell that is generally self-serving or just plain selfish. Of course, we do have to look after ourselves, and this is by no means wrong—but not at the expense of others. So if the object of your desire is a friend's spouse, some fast money to pay off gambling debts, or a way of getting in good with an elderly person so he will leave you everything he owns—well, you need to think this over before casting a spell.

Admittedly, ours is a very self-centered society. We live in an age where we are encouraged to promote only ourselves, and every book we see is how we can get ahead using the latest gimmicks or techniques. Perhaps this explains why those who are self-serving tend to end up claiming the biggest prizes, not because they're the best, but because they are the ones willing to stoop to certain tactics, whether ethical or not, to achieve their goals. This should come as no surprise, since our culture promotes it. Although this is not *always* the case, it happens frequently enough to place obstacles in the way of people who are actually more talented or deserving.

So how do we know if we're more deserving?

Objectively, we probably don't. Most of us live in the space of our own views where it's hard to see the views of another—especially if we don't like that person in the first place. Dislike for something or someone is always a devilish temptation when it comes to casting spells. For this reason, almost any spell requires a great deal of contemplation and forethought. We should always be just, even to our enemies. Even so, some of our most generous goals can run into serious blocks. Our loftiest dreams can be frustrated by what seem to be insurmountable hurdles. And if this goes on long enough, we can become bitter, coming to believe that life is basically unfair, and that luck is on the side of those willing to cheat, scheme, or grovel.

It doesn't have to be that way.

No one ever said that in order to be a good person, we must be passive and accept whatever misfortune comes our way. Ideally, we should make the most of our lives, all the while helping others make the most of theirs. This is where the Spell to Attain Your Heart's Desire can be of assistance. Although this is a rather general spell that can address a multitude of issues, it is also a powerful one, getting to the heart of your matter of concern.

For this spell, you will need to set up an altar that can be used over a period of seven days. I would suggest you keep this altar area hidden away from others during the duration of this spell for practical purposes. It is also essential that you not discuss your spell with anyone until your casting ritual has been completed.

Why? Too much talk or discussion can dissipate the energy behind your spell rather than reinforce it. I'm sure you've met individuals who are always talking of big plans, but they never seem to get around to accomplishing what they dream of doing because they are too busy talking about it. The same holds true of spells. Perhaps the spirits know that this is a type of boasting, and they sabotage the outcome just to teach us witches a lesson! At any rate, you will want to keep your ritual a secret for a while as a precaution.

A square, dark cloth that can be folded into the shape of a triangle will be needed for your altar. You will also need a red, a green, and a black candle, as well as two feet of narrow ribbon or cord in any color you choose. The ribbon or cord will later be used in your knotting ritual magic. (What's a knotting ritual? Stay tuned—you'll soon learn.)

Although not mandatory, you may wish to purchase or make seven charms or pendants that have special meaning for you. Charms for charm bracelets can be found in inexpensive accessory shops and other retail stores. You may want to choose charms or symbols that have special meaning for the spell you are about to cast. Zodiac symbols of those involved, moons, stars, planets, animals, dream catchers, and flowers make wonderful charms. Gold or silver, or a mixture of both, are also very nice. Crystal enthusiasts may want to use small crystals instead of charms.

To complete your ritual area, you will need to select the following seven runes: the Eye Rune, the Sun Rune, the Moon Rune, the Man Rune, the Romance Rune, the Woman Rune and the Star Rune. These are the stones that hold the most magnetism and tend to draw toward you what you need. These runes have opposite natures, which create a tension that both pulls and attracts, increasing their magnetism.

For the structure of your altar, we turn to Ancient Egypt for inspiration. The Egyptians were once the most powerful magicians in the world. Every aspect of their lives was based upon their unique brand of spirituality and their use of ceremonial magic. Since strong measures need strong magic, we will use the Egyptian symbol of power to enhance our spell.

Take your square cloth and fold it into a triangle. This should work as a facsimile of an Egyptian pyramid. Place the cloth on the table. Moving from left to right, put the Man Rune on the bottom left of your pyramid, place the Romance Rune in the center, and the Woman Rune to the right. These will serve as the bottom level of your pyramid. Moving upward, place the Sun Rune to the left, representing the King's chambers of wisdom, and the Moon Rune to the right, representing the Queen's chambers of inspiration. The Eye Rune at the top of the pyramid is indicative of the All-knowing, All-seeing Godhead, Goddess, or Creator. It makes no difference what gender you choose. Directly left of the King's chamber and the Sun Rune, you will need to place the Star Rune, representing the constellation Sirius, or Dog Star. (Allow a space of six or seven inches. See diagram on page 195.) Sirius held important meaning for the Ancient Egyptians because this is where they believed Pharaohs traveled after death to continue their kingly reign amongst the stars.

Now begin setting up your candles. The red candle goes beside the Man Rune, representing the active energies of manhood and the planet Mars. The green candle should be placed beside the Woman Rune, suggesting the procreative energies of the female and the planet Venus.

Place the black candle at the top. Black is used to neutralize and focus all of the energies into one direction because black represents an absence waiting to be filled by the light of our ideals and desires. Before lighting your candles, however, make certain your ribbon is close by for the knotting magic.

Look at your altar and compare it to the diagram to make sure everything is in order. At the bottom of your pyramid, you may want to place some items that hold special meaning for you. These can include Egyptian ankhs or scarabs, Native American dream-catchers or totem animals, sticks of incense, sacred oils or whatever seems right for the moment.

Before beginning your ritual, say a silent prayer of protection. Upon completion of your prayer, imagine yourself swathed in a robe of white light. Now think hard about your wish. Visualize the way in which this wish can come true. Ask yourself how this wish can not only benefit you, but also benefit others. You may proceed to light your candles, moving from left to right and then directly above the pyramid. These are the words to begin your spell with:

The time is near. I light the fire,
to bring to me what I desire.
On wind and cloud, over storm or sea,
bring me what belongs to me!

Take your ribbon and begin to make the first knot while concentrating on your goal. You may tie a little charm into the first knot if you wish. Focus powerfully upon your desire while tying your ribbon or cord. These are the words you need to say:

> I take this string. I make the knot,
> to bind the (object of desire) to my heart.
> I take this cord. I make the knot.
> Draw to me what I have sought!

Loop your ribbon in a circle around the Star Rune.

Relax for a moment. Consider the beauty and liveliness of your altar. Gaze into the flickering light of your candles. Now move your focus to the Eye Rune. Again, visualize your wish. Make the object of your desire a reality in your mind's eye. Reflect on your wish for a few minutes. (At this time you may begin to sense the presence of spirits in the room. Be aware. But do not be afraid.)

Now say this:

> The time is right. I keep the fire.
> Bring fast to me what I desire!
> Over storm, over earth and sea.
> The God(dess)s say it belongs to me.
> So shall it be!

Meditate on your goal. Go over every aspect of your wish. Watch your candle flames dance, sputter, surge freely, and move. The flames represent the fiery energy you are willing to put forth to make your desire a reality. Sometimes you will pick up on psychic impressions while in front of your altar or when in a meditative state. It would be wise to write these down immediately after your ritual.

Now blow out your candles one by one. After the candles have sufficiently cooled, you may want to place a clean cardboard box or

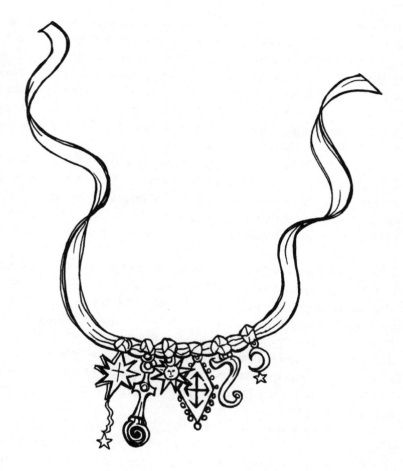

cloth over your altar, since you will be working with it over the next six days.

Tomorrow you will want to repeat this ritual by adding a second knot and charm to your ribbon. You will want to work on this spell for seven days, tying seven knots, and repeating the incantation seven times. At the end of seven days, your spell may not yet be complete. You may wish to take your magickal knotted ribbon with its charms or crystals, and wear it as a sacred necklace. Don't be surprised to find that this magickal-knot necklace is one of the most psychically charged pieces of jewelry you've ever worn. After all, it contains the power behind your hopes and dreams, since it is infused with your innate psychic powers. During the day, you may want to touch this necklace to remind yourself of your goal and to fantasize freely about the wish or desire. Use your magickal-knot necklace as a reminder of the way you want your life to be in the future. Think of this daily.

Within the next six to eight months, you should see powerful changes in your life resulting as the outcome of this spell. You may repeat this spell once a month, but it is suggested you try it only when the moon is in a waxing and growing state. Above all else, leave your heart and mind open.

The Witch's Runes can be used for any kind of spell or blessing that you have in mind. The possibilities are limitless. However, spells may not be the most important work you have to do as an attuned, magickal person. Sometimes you might wait and see what the universe has to offer before making a decision to cast a spell. After all, the strongest magick exists in your ability to give love and kindness—with no strings attached. You can impart no greater blessing. You can cast no greater spell. The greater your love, the more power and influence you attract into your life.

As you continue to work with the Witch's Runes, ponder their messages and their meanings. See how they relate to yourself and others. Experiment with their unusual brand of knowledge. Learn to live the wisdom of the ancient Witch—the one who exists in the nighttime flow of mysterious beauty.

Accept these Witch's Runes. They are a gift. Reclaim the powers that live in you. It is you who called them forth.

They are yours now. Use them wisely and well.

Printed in Great Britain
by Amazon